CLASSICAL COMICS
TEACHING RESOURCE PACK

Making Shakespeare accessible for teachers and students

Suitable for teaching ages 10–17

Written by: Kornel Kossuth
US Adaptation: Joe Sutliff Sanders

CLASSICAL COMICS
TEACHING RESOURCE PACK
A Midsummer Night's Dream

Perfect bound edition published 2013
First published 2011

Published by: Classical Comics
Copyright ©2011 Classical Comics Ltd.

Written by:	Kornel Kossuth
US Adaptation:	Joe Sutliff Sanders
Characters & Artwork:	Kat Nicholson & Jason Cardy
Design & Layout:	Jo Wheeler & Carl Andrews
Editor in Chief:	Clive Bryant

The rights of Kornel Kossuth, Joe Sutliff Sanders, Kat Nicholson and
Jason Cardy to be identified as the artists of this work have been
asserted in accordance with the Copyright, Designs and Patents Act
1988 sections 77 and 78.

Acknowledgments: Every effort has been made to trace copyright
holders of material reproduced in this book. Any rights not
acknowledged here will be acknowledged in subsequent editions if
notice is given to Classical Comics Ltd.

All enquiries should be addressed to:
Classical Comics Ltd.
PO Box 16310
Birmingham
B30 9EL
United Kingdom

education@classicalcomics.com
www.classicalcomics.com

ISBN: 978-1-907127-76-2

Printed in the USA

CONTENTS

INTRODUCTION

WELCOME TO *A MIDSUMMER NIGHT'S DREAM* TEACHING RESOURCE FROM CLASSICAL COMICS.

This resource has manifold aims, which I hope it achieves:

- It is designed to be easy to use, giving teachers who have never worked with *A Midsummer Night's Dream* an in-depth guide on a range of activities they can deploy. The approach is therefore comprehensive, and this resource gives you a set of ready-to-teach lessons that need little preparation.

- The division of activities into chapters allows teachers more familiar with the text and its teaching to pick and choose the activities they want. A brief introduction to each topic, designed to kick-start thoughts on the theme, helps teachers re-cap their knowledge.

- Most importantly, this resource aims to provide a variety of activities that stimulate enjoyable learning for pupils aged 10-17. Each topic contains lesson ideas and photocopiable worksheets. For those tasks that involve a more closed response, teacher answer sheets are provided at the back of the book. Of course, the answers provided are mostly suggestions only and by no means exhaustive. Where there is no teacher sheet, the task is designed to be more exploratory, with the emphasis on pupils being able to explain their findings rather than guessing what the pre-fabricated "right" answer might be.

Although designed with the Classical Comics version of *A Midsummer Night's Dream* in mind, this resource can be used successfully with the traditional text.

If you would like to send feedback or suggest ways to improve this book, please email **education@classicalcomics.com** – your thoughts and input are always appreciated.

Kornel Kossuth

THE BACKGROUND OF
A MIDSUMMER NIGHT'S DREAM

INTRODUCTION

Each Shakespeare play is enjoyable in its own right, either as a performance or as a text. However, a closer look at the background of a play, and in particular the era in which it was written, can be useful to find out what themes are present within it. In this context, a look at Shakespeare's life and what was happening at the time he wrote his plays can yield interesting information.

A Midsummer Night's Dream is of particular interest as its main plot-line is not based on any one definite source (although some parts of the play are based on other stories), while its theme is similar to that of *Romeo and Juliet* – a play Shakespeare almost certainly wrote around the same time.

There are a number of ways pupils can engage with the life and times of Shakespeare and the background of *A Midsummer Night's Dream*:

- A number of people contend that *A Midsummer Night's Dream* was written for an aristocratic wedding that Queen Elizabeth I herself may have attended. There are a number of clues in the text that could support this point of view. Based on textual evidence and using the essay framework, pupils might argue that the play was first performed at a private wedding.

- The pupils can also use the theme essay framework to explore how historical and sociological events may have influenced the plot and themes of the play.

- It was traditional at the end of a play, especially comedies, to ask for the audience's approval and to apologize for any shortcomings. In *A Midsummer Night's Dream* Puck does this in the epilogue, but with a marked difference: Puck expressly states that if the audience didn't enjoy the play they should imagine they had dreamt it. To what extent is this an original ending when compared to other epilogues, and in what way does it continue the play's preoccupation with dreams?

- In its plot-line of the Mechanicals, Shakespeare gives us a behind-the-scenes glimpse of how theatre worked in his day. Pupils could research the limitations of theatre in the Elizabethan and Jacobean era and how plays were performed in those days (costumes, scenery and props). A good place to start is the New Globe Theatre in London.

Of course, any work done on the play's background should tie in with work done in lessons and serve to enrich the pupils' understanding of the play.

SHAKESPEARE'S TIMES
HISTORICAL AND SOCIOLOGICAL INFLUENCES

A Midsummer Night's Dream is one of the few plays whose main plot-line is not based on a specific source. While Shakespeare was definitely influenced by Ovid's *Metamorphoses*, North's *Life of Theseus*, Seneca's *Hippolytus* and Chaucer's *Canterbury Tales*, none is a sufficient source in itself for the whole of the play's action. A number of the play's themes are rooted in contemporary events and preoccupations. Love and marriage are central, which would make sense if the play was originally written to be performed at a wedding, as many historians believe.

Love and Marriage

In Elizabethan England, marriage was very much a social contract entered into between two people of equal standing, with the purpose of producing an heir and thus securing the family name and wealth for another generation. This was true mainly of the aristocracy, but it was also true of other classes. Although marriage had to be entered into of one's own free will, love was not usually of primary concern. If anything, it was a bonus. Parents and friends would have had a large influence in selecting a prospective partner. Indeed, parents would have to consent to a marriage. However, if there were no financial or social obstacles, this consent was rarely withheld. In this sense, Egeus is not typical of the Elizabethan era, especially as Lysander and Demetrius are of equal standing.

While society frowned on single men and women meeting unless they were "a couple," there were certain ritualized meetings to help youths come together (people usually married in their twenties). A number of celebrations, like "maying," allowed young people to get to know one another in group situations. At such festivals the youths would sing, dance and play games of varying intimacy. Shakespeare suggests that the play, as far as the lovers are concerned, may be an extended form of "maying," and by the end of it (at the end of Act IV), the lovers have paired off into their couples and are ready for marriage that is now based on love.

Stagecraft

Although a number of Shakespeare's plays have a play within a play, *A Midsummer Night's Dream* is the only one that allows us to look behind the scenes. Admittedly, the performance is not a professional one, but it is hard not to see parallels between how Shakespeare presents the Mechanicals and actual Elizabethan theatre troupes.

There is one specific reference to a true stage event in the play: when discussing Snout's part as lion (III.1), the Mechanicals are afraid the lion might scare the ladies in the audience. In Edinburgh, in 1594, plans to have a chariot drawn in by lions at a pageant marking the baptism of Prince Henry were abandoned because the beasts might strike fear in the onlookers. So it is probably safe to say that when writing about the Mechanicals, Shakespeare was at least satirizing his contemporaries and competitors.

Plays in Shakespeare's days were performed in costume of the period with very little scenery. It was up to the language of the play to recreate the world and make the audience "see" the scenery that wasn't there. In this respect, the Mechanicals' insistence on bringing in a real wall and real moonshine is out of keeping with Elizabethan stage practice, and thus is ludicrous.

We do get a sense of the confusion a rehearsal could bring. Actors did not have the whole play in front of them, but only their parts and their cues. Before the first run through or without the help of the director, they would have had very little idea what the play was about *. Therefore Quince has to explain the play not only for the audience's benefit, but also the players'. While Flute can, in his nervousness, read the whole of his part without noticing that he is reading past his own cues.

What is also unusual here is a group of laymen amateurs performing in front of aristocracy. Theatre was either performed by professional companies, such as Shakespeare's, or as pageants by amateur aristocrats in front of other aristocrats. This may be Shakespeare telling us precisely what he thinks about his competitors, or simply a device to heighten the comedy.

* for a truly superb insight into how plays were rehearsed in Shakespeare's day, get a copy of *Secrets of Acting Shakespeare* by Patrick Tucker of the Original Shakespeare Company.

Dreams

For a play that has "dream" in its title, there is remarkably little dreaming going on. Although dreams are often mentioned and many characters at various stages believe they must have been dreaming (at the end the audience is asked to make believe the whole play was "but a dream"), there is only one actual dream in *A Midsummer Night's Dream* – the one dreamt by Hermia after Lysander has left her at the end of Act II.2. Elizabethan England differentiated between two different types of dreams. The first were those that presented hopes or fears, like a lover dreaming of her loved one, or a hunter dreaming of killing a prize animal. These dreams presented what we would now call "day residue" and are, as such, unspectacular and of no further interest or significance. The second category were predictive dreams that contained some message about future events. What makes prediction tricky is that often the visions are metaphorical rather than literal (so, instead of dreaming of a murder, the dreamer might dream that a certain animal that represents the victim is killed).

As Hermia was not worried when she lay down to sleep, her dream must be rated as predictive. While metaphorical, it is not difficult to interpret. But what about all the other references to dreams? You might explore what kinds of dreams they are, and the meaning behind them.

Fairies, the Moon and the Weather

When Oberon and Titania meet for the first time, Titania explains that the current turmoil in nature is due to the conflict between them. While fairies are not customarily responsible for the weather, there were a number of years in which the weather was considered abnormal. The years 1594-1596 all had extraordinary summers: wet and cold like winter, with regular flooding, pointing to a dislocation of the seasons just as Titania laments.

With the exception of their influence on the weather, Shakespeare's fairies (and Puck in particular) are very much creatures of rural folklore. Apart from a penchant for causing mischief, they are inherently neither good nor evil. Puck will help those who are kind to him, even though he plays pranks on others. The types of prank point to things going inexplicably wrong in an agricultural community requiring some unseen being – such as a fairy – to be invented as scapegoat. Their size seems to vary, as Titania has no problem embracing the transformed Bottom, but at the same time they battle with bats and bees, and can hide in acorns.

If fairies are considered to be demons (as many pagan gods were believed to be), then they would be able to influence the weather, as ruining crops was a prime occupation of witches and demons. Indeed, many of Puck's pranks could be seen as the work of a witch. While King of Scotland, James VI (who became James I of England when Queen Elizabeth died) wrote a book on witches, *Daemonologie* (1597). In it he expressly stated that fairies were a type of demon. He also specified that they followed Diana, the goddess of the moon. This keys in directly to the countless references to the moon and the strange, magical goings-on in the moonlit woods.

PUCK'S EPILOGUE
"No epilogue, I pray you"

In a number of plays, mostly the comedies, Shakespeare adds an epilogue at the end of the action. The epilogue is usually delivered by one of the characters, and its purpose is to apologize for the insufficiencies of the play, seeking the audience's goodwill and approval through its applause. As such, it is quite a standard piece.

However in *A Midsummer Night's Dream*, Shakespeare manages to provide an interesting variation on this idea. While the epilogue sounds conventional enough, its affinity with the content of the play itself led Shakespeare to provide in it a brilliant *coup de théâtre*. In a play in which dreams are so often mentioned, but seldom dreamt, the playwright asks the audience to imagine the play was "but a dream" if they didn't like it. This is a significant shift from other epilogues.

With the aid of other Shakespearean epilogues, and the comparison chart, pupils can explore the ending of *A Midsummer Night's Dream* before comparing it to those of the other plays. Although three other epilogues are presented, it is suggested that pupils compare the epilogue of *A Midsummer Night's Dream* with two other epilogues of their choice.

THE ENDING OF *A MIDSUMMER NIGHT'S DREAM*

TASK:

Compare two of the following epilogues to Puck's epilogue.

From *The Tempest*	From *All's Well That Ends Well*	From *As You Like It*
PROSPERO Now my charms are all o'erthrown, And what strength I have's mine own, Which is most faint: now, 'tis true, I must be here confin'd by you, Or sent to Naples. Let me not, Since I have my dukedom got, And pardon'd the deceiver, dwell In this bare island, by your spell; But release me from my bands, With the help of your good hands. Gentle breath of yours my sails Must fill, or else my project fails, Which was to please. Now I want Spirits to enforce, art to enchant; And my ending is despair, Unless I be reliev'd by prayer, Which pierces so, that it assaults Mercy itself, and frees all faults. As you from crimes would pardon'd be, Let your indulgence set me free.	KING The king's a beggar now the play is done: All is well ended, if this suit be won, That you express content; which we will pay, With strife to please you, day exceeding day: Ours be your patience then, and yours our parts; Your gentle hands lend us, and take our hearts.	ROSALIND It is not the fashion to see the lady the epilogue; but it is no more unhandsome than to see the lord the prologue. If it be true that good wine needs no bush, 'tis true that a good play needs no epilogue; yet to good wine they do use good bushes, and good plays prove the better by the help of good epilogues. What a case am I in then, that am neither a good epilogue nor cannot insinuate with you in the behalf of a good play? I am not furnished like a beggar, therefore to beg will not become me: my way is to conjure you; and I'll begin with the women. I charge you, O women! for the love you bear to men, to like as much of this play as please you: and I charge you, O men! for the love you bear to women -- as I perceive by your simpering, none of you hates them -- that between you and the women, the play may please. If I were a woman, I would kiss as many of you as had beards that pleased me, complexions that liked me and breaths that I defied not: and, I am sure, as many as have good beards, or good faces, or sweet breaths, will, for my kind offer, when I make curtsy, bid me farewell.

Prospero from Classical Comics' *The Tempest*.
Artwork by: Jon Haward and Gary Erskine

9

THE ENDING OF *A MIDSUMMER NIGHT'S DREAM*

TASK:

Use the following table first to examine Puck's epilogue and then to compare it with two others.

Question	A Midsummer Night's Dream	The Tempest	All's Well That Ends Well	As You Like It
Who delivers the Prologue?				
Is the actor in character?				
How is the character trying to persuade the audience to clap?				
How does the epilogue relate to the rest of the play?				

SCENE-BY-SCENE SYNOPSIS

Act I Scene 1

Theseus, Duke of Athens, is impatient to marry Hippolyta, the conquered Queen of the Amazons, but he still has to wait four more days.

Egeus comes to the duke to complain that his daughter, Hermia, does not want to obey him and marry Demetrius. Instead, she loves Lysander. According to Athenian law, Hermia must either marry her father's choice of husband, be executed, or live the life of a nun, away from all men. Theseus gives Hermia four days to decide.

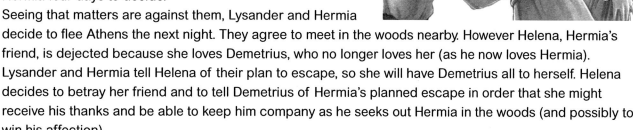

Seeing that matters are against them, Lysander and Hermia decide to flee Athens the next night. They agree to meet in the woods nearby. However Helena, Hermia's friend, is dejected because she loves Demetrius, who no longer loves her (as he now loves Hermia). Lysander and Hermia tell Helena of their plan to escape, so she will have Demetrius all to herself. Helena decides to betray her friend and to tell Demetrius of Hermia's planned escape in order that she might receive his thanks and be able to keep him company as he seeks out Hermia in the woods (and possibly to win his affection).

Act I Scene 2

Quince, Bottom, Snug, Flute, Snout and Starveling (the so-called "Mechanicals"), all simple workmen of Athens, meet to discuss a play they want to perform for the Duke's wedding. Although Quince is their leader, Bottom keeps taking over; in particular, he wants to play every part of their chosen play, *Pyramus and Thisbe*, although his role is to be that of Pyramus, an unfortunate lover. Flute plays Thisbe, his lady-love. The other workmen are to play the lovers' parents, with the exception of Snug the

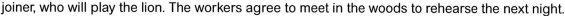

joiner, who will play the lion. The workers agree to meet in the woods to rehearse the next night.

Act II Scene 1

A fairy and Robin Goodfellow, or "Puck," meet in the woods as both are preparing the arrival of their respective rulers, Titania and Oberon, queen and king of the fairies. Oberon and Titania have fallen out over an Indian boy whom Titania has adopted, and whom Oberon wants as a page. Because of their quarrel, nature is in turmoil and all the seasons are muddled up. Titania refuses to give up the boy or to rejoin Oberon. The fairy king decides to make her pay and asks Puck to find a magical flower. When the juice of the flower is dripped into the eyes of someone asleep, it makes them fall in love with the first thing they see when they wake. Oberon plans to use this to make Titania fall in love with some horrible creature.

While Puck is gone, Helena and Demetrius pass through the woods, searching for Hermia and Lysander. Oberon watches Demetrius spurn Helena and makes a promise that Demetrius will love her soon. Puck returns with the magical flower, and Oberon tells him to find the Athenian and administer the flower juice while he sleeps, so that he may fall in love with the girl he is with.

SCENE-BY-SCENE SYNOPSIS

Act II Scene 2

Titania, surrounded by her fairy court, goes to sleep. While asleep, Oberon puts some of the juice from the flower in her eyes. Hermia and Lysander appear in the woods, having lost their way. They decide to wait till dawn before proceeding further. Instead of sleeping close together, Hermia asks Lysander to sleep farther away from her, as modesty requires. While they are asleep, Puck happens upon the two. He thinks these are the two Athenians Oberon talked about, and he squeezes the juice of the flower into Lysander's eyes. When Helena comes along, having been abandoned by Demetrius, Lysander wakes to see her and, under the flower's magical power, falls in love with her. Helena thinks Lysander is mocking her and leaves. Lysander follows, leaving Hermia asleep alone. She wakes and finds she is alone, having had a nightmare in which a snake eats her heart.

Act III Scene 1

The Mechanicals meet in the woods to rehearse their play. They begin by discussing whether their play might frighten the ladies before rehearsing their lines. Puck watches the laborers make a mess of things and decides to have some fun with them. While Bottom is sent "off stage" and away from the others, Puck conjures a donkey's head onto him. When his fellow workers see him they flee, leaving him alone, singing to keep himself company. His singing wakes Titania, who has been sleeping nearby, and because of the flower juice administered by Oberon, she falls in love with him. She orders her fairies to wait on him and then leads him to her bed.

Act III Scene 2

Puck tells Oberon all that has happened. Oberon is pleased, but when Demetrius and Hermia enter, Oberon realizes that Puck has bewitched the wrong man. Hermia believes Demetrius has killed Lysander, but he denies bringing harm to him. She leaves Demetrius, and, exhausted, he lies down to sleep. Oberon applies the flower to his eyes and orders Puck to bring Helena to him. Helena enters, followed by a lovesick Lysander. When Demetrius awakes, he too is now in love with Helena. Helena thinks the two men are mocking her. Hermia then arrives, and Lysander tells her that he no longer loves her. Helena thinks that Hermia is also out to make fun of her, but Hermia accuses her friend of having bewitched Lysander.

Lysander and Demetrius decide to fight over their right to Helena and leave. The two women leave, too (separately). Oberon reprimands Puck and orders him to set things right by dripping the antidote into Lysander's eye. Puck casts a dense fog over the woods and separates the two men, who are trying to find each other so that they might fight. He leads both astray until, exhausted, they separately fall asleep. The two women also find their way to the area and fall asleep in the woods, exhausted by the night's events. Puck anoints Lysander's eyes with the antidote.

SCENE-BY-SCENE SYNOPSIS

Act IV Scene 1

Titania continues to dote on Bottom with his ass's head. They fall asleep together. Oberon, who has meanwhile received the changeling boy from Titania, frees her from the spell, and she wakes. She sees Bottom with the donkey's head and realizes what has happened. Titania and Oberon are reconciled and decide to bless Theseus's wedding together (although we never learn the fate of the changeling boy!).

A short while later, while out hunting, Theseus, Hippolyta and Egeus stumble upon the four lovers, who are sleeping in close proximity, unbeknownst to them due to the dense fog the previous night. As best they can, they tell the Duke what has happened. Demetrius is now in love with Helena (either genuinely, or possibly due to the juice from the magical flower). Although Egeus still wants Demetrius to marry Hermia, Theseus overrules him and decides that the two happy couples shall marry together with him and Hippolyta.

After all have left, Bottom wakes up as his normal self (with his human head) but at a complete loss to say what has happened.

Act IV Scene 2

Without Bottom, the Mechanicals despair as they cannot hope to stage the play without their leading actor. All their hopes for fame and honor are dashed. Then, suddenly, Bottom arrives and urges them to prepare for their performance.

Act V Scene 1

Hippolyta and Theseus marvel at the story of the four lovers. When presented with the choice of plays to while away the time until the night, Theseus – despite the protests of his master of revels, Philostrate – chooses the Mechanicals' play of *Pyramus and Thisbe*.

During the play, the Athenian youths mock the labourers, who overact and misread their lines. In the play, Pyramus and Thisbe are two lovers whose parents don't approve of their love. They communicate through a chink in the wall and agree to meet outside the town. Thisbe is first there and is surprised by a lion. She runs away, but leaves her scarf in its maw. Pyramus then arrives and, seeing the mauled scarf, thinks Thisbe is dead and kills himself. When Thisbe returns she sees the dead Pyramus and kills herself out of grief. Theseus is pleased with the play, and all retire. The play over, the celebrations ended for the day, and everyone in bed, Oberon, Titania and their fairies fly through the house, blessing it and the couples within it.

Epilogue

Puck remains alone and asks that the audience, if displeased, imagine that what they saw was just a dream. If, however, they are pleased, he asks for their approval through clapping.

COMPREHENSION
ACT I

Fill in the blanks using the words provided.
You may use a word once only, and you may not need to use them all.

Theseus, the _____ of Athens, can hardly wait to get married to _____, the Queen of the

_____, whom he conquered in _____. Egeus disrupts their preparations and complains

that his daughter, _____, will not obey his instructions and marry _____ because she loves

_____ instead. Theseus tells Hermia that, on the day of the royal wedding, she must decide either

to marry as her father wishes, be executed, or become a _____ forever. Lysander and Hermia

bewail their bad fortune and decide to _____ from _____. They tell Hermia's friend Helena

all about their intentions. _____ was once loved by Demetrius, before he loved Hermia. She still

loves Demetrius and secretly decides to tell him of the lovers' _____ to leave the town, in the hope

of receiving some _____ .

Meanwhile, a group of simple _____ from Athens are planning to perform a _____ for the

Duke's _____ celebrations. They plan on staging *Pyramus and* _____, with Bottom as

_____ and _____ as Thisbe, although _____ wants to play all the parts in the

play. They decide to meet in the _____ the next night to rehearse.

King	**Helena**	**woods**	**city**	**Lysander**
Pyramus	**Syracuse**	**thanks**	**Duke**	**Bottom**
flee	**wanderers**	**kisses**	**Centaurs**	**nun**
Amazons	**workmen**	**Athens**	**Egeus**	**dance**
Flute	**priestess**	**plan**	**wedding**	**Thisbe**
Hermia	**play**	**Hippolyta**	**Demetrius**	**battle**

COMPREHENSION
ACT II

Fill in the blanks using the words provided.
You may use a word once only, and you may not need to use them all.

Robin Goodfellow, otherwise known as _____ , meets a _____ in the woods. Both Titania and Oberon, the Queen and the King of the fairies, plan to be in the _____ that night. However, the two are in conflict because _____ has an Indian child that _____ wants, and she _____ to give it up. As a result of their _____ , nature is in _____ . Oberon is prepared to end the fight if Titania gives him the child. Her refusal makes Oberon vow to make her pay for her _____ . He orders Puck to search out a _____ , the juice of which makes people fall in love with the next thing they _____ when they wake, after it has been applied to the _____ . Oberon wants to make sure that Titania wakes up when something _____ is near.

While Puck is gone, Oberon watches Demetrius and _____ walk through the woods in search of _____ and Hermia. Demetrius continues to push Helena away. When Puck comes back to Oberon with the flower, in an attempt to set things right between Demetrius and Helena, he tells Puck to _____ the Athenian's eyes with the flower juice so that he will _____ the girl he _____ .

Elsewhere, Titania falls asleep, surrounded by her _____ . While asleep, Oberon smears some of the flower's _____ onto her eyes.

In another part of the wood, Hermia and Lysander have lost their way; tired, they decide to sleep where they are. As they are not yet _____ , Hermia insists that they sleep _____ . Puck, seeing them, thinks these are the two his master talked about, and he applies the juice onto _____ eyes. Helena stumbles into the area and wakes him. The magic of the flower has its effect, and he falls in love with her. Helena runs off, but Lysander _____ her. After dreaming that a _____ was eating her heart, Hermia wakes up alone.

cily	hate	see	old enough	quarrel
disobedience	flower	eyes	anoint	vile
juice	turmoil	Puck	woods	Oberon
Demetrius	Lysander	together	fairy	spurned
snake	follows	love	married	Demetrius's
Hermia	Titania	refuses	apart	fairy-court
potion	Lysander's	harmony	thought	Helena

COMPREHENSION
ACT III

Fill in the blanks using the words provided.
You may use a word once only, and you may not need to use them all.

Puck watches the _____ rehearse their play and decides to have some fun with them. He puts a spell on _____ so that his head becomes a _____ . When his friends see him, they run away. Left by himself, he _____ to cheer himself up. The noise wakes _____ , who _____ with him.

Puck reports all he has done to _____ , who is _____ .
_____ and Hermia enter, Hermia accusing him of having killed _____ . Oberon realizes Puck has made a _____ . While Demetrius sleeps, exhausted from the night's events, Oberon puts the love juice on his eyes.
_____ enters, followed by Lysander. Waking under the power of the potion, Demetrius sees Helena and falls in love with her; now both men _____ over her. _____ returns to the scene and accuses Helena of having _____ Lysander. The two men go off to fight, and the two women leave separately.

Oberon is _____ at Puck and tells him to set things right. Puck conjures up a dense _____ in the wood and leads the two men _____ . When they both fall asleep from _____ , Puck drips an _____ into _____ eyes. The two women, also tired from the night's happenings, arrive at the scene and, thinking they are alone, fall _____ , too.

Oberon	**bewitched**	**asleep**	**elephant**	**astray**
down	**killed**	**delighted**	**falls in love**	**Titania**
Hermia	**talks**	**Flute**	**potion**	**angry**
mistake	**antidote**	**Demetrius**	**fight**	**Lysander's**
Bottom	**Demetrius's**	**Mechanicals**	**Helena**	**sings**
donkey's	**exhaustion**	**fog**	**Theseus**	**Lysander**

COMPREHENSION
ACT IV

Fill in the blanks using the words provided.
You may use a word once only, and you may not need to use them all.

_____ continues to be in love with the donkey-headed Bottom and asks her fairies to pander to his every _____ . Oberon, who has meanwhile _____ the Indian child from Titania, releases her from her _____ . Titania wakes to see Bottom with the _____ head and realizes she has not been _____ . The two make up and decide to _____ Theseus's wedding.

_____ and his court are out _____ in the morning, when they stumble upon the four lovers, who wake up to find that while _____ loves _____ again, _____ now loves _____ . _____ still wants Hermia to marry Demetrius, but Theseus overrules him, seeing as the four are now _____ . Theseus decides that the two _____ will _____ together with him and Hippolyta.

After they have left the scene, _____ also wakes up, returned to his normal state and as _____ again; but he cannot say what happened to him.

Back in Athens, the Mechanics are _____ without Bottom as they cannot _____ the play without him. Suddenly he bursts in, and they are _____ and have _____ again that their performance will go ahead.

Helena	**overjoyed**	**taken**	**spell**	**wish**
Egeus	**matched**	**Oberon**	**Demetrius**	**couples**
marry	**live**	**ruin**	**Theseus**	**Lysander**
bless	**Puck**	**donkey**	**hunting**	**hope**
dreaming	**himself**	**given**	**sleeping**	**Hermia**
Titania	**distraught**	**Bottom**	**perform**	**Hippolyta**

17

COMPREHENSION
ACT V

Fill in the blanks using the words provided.
You may use a word once only, and you may not need to use them all.

Theseus and _____ are not sure what to make of the lovers' _____ of the night's

happenings. Philostrate, the master of the Duke's _____ and entertainment, presents Theseus with a

number of plays to _____ away the evening until bedtime. He chooses the Mechanicals' play of

Pyramus and Thisbe.

All through the _____ , the Athenians make fun of the _____ and poor acting of the

Mechanicals. Peter Quince, as prologue, gets his _____ all wrong in his lines, saying

the _____ of what he means. In the play, _____ (played by _____) and Thisbe

(played by _____) live next to each other and love one another, although their _____ are

against their love. They _____ through a chink or hole in the great wall that separates them, played

by Snout. They agree to meet in secret outside the _____ . Thisbe arrives _____ at their

meeting place and is _____ by a _____ (played by Snug). She flees but leaves her scarf,

which is _____ by the lion. When Pyramus arrives, he

sees the mauled scarf and, believing that his beloved has been

killed, _____ himself. Thisbe _____ and sees

the _____ Pyramus; distraught, she kills herself, too.

_____ is _____ with the play and gives praise to

the actors. After the play, they all go off to their _____ .

When all have left, Oberon, Titania and their _____ fly through the house and _____ its

inhabitants.

Finally, at the end of the play, Puck enters, alone, and asks for _____ or, if the audience did not

enjoy the play, for them to imagine it was only a _____ .

parents	**Pyramus**	**antics**	**revels**	**while**
killed	**applause**	**fairies**	**rooms**	**performance**
Hippolyta	**frightened**	**Flute**	**kills**	**bless**
opposite	**city**	**lion**	**Egeus**	**Bottom**
punctuation	**pleased**	**mauled**	**returns**	**Theseus**
account	**dead**	**dream**	**communicate**	**first**

THE DIFFERENT WORLDS OF
A MIDSUMMER NIGHT'S DREAM
"In the wood, a league without the town"

In *A Midsummer Night's Dream*, Shakespeare brings together three different worlds and three different plot-lines. First are the Athenian court and the lovers in a plot revolving around love, marriage and finding the perfect partner. Set against this is the second world, that of the Mechanicals staging a story of tragic love. Finally, Shakespeare also presents us with the fairy world, with its troubled king and queen.

The diagram below shows how Shakespeare structures and interweaves the three worlds into a coherent whole. Fill in the squares, briefly detailing the events that take place. The first one is done for you.

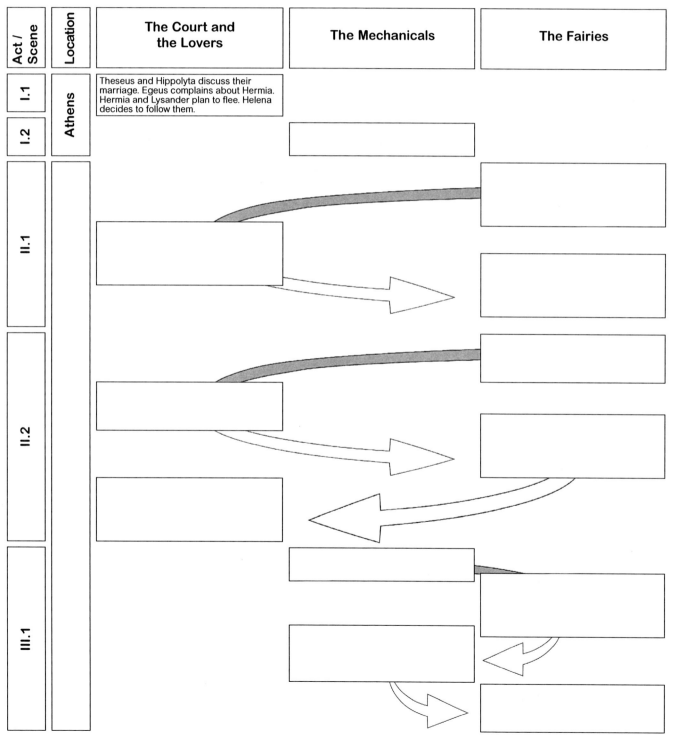

Act / Scene	Location	The Court and the Lovers	The Mechanicals	The Fairies
I.1	Athens	Theseus and Hippolyta discuss their marriage. Egeus complains about Hermia. Hermia and Lysander plan to flee. Helena decides to follow them.		
I.2				
II.1				
II.2				
III.1				

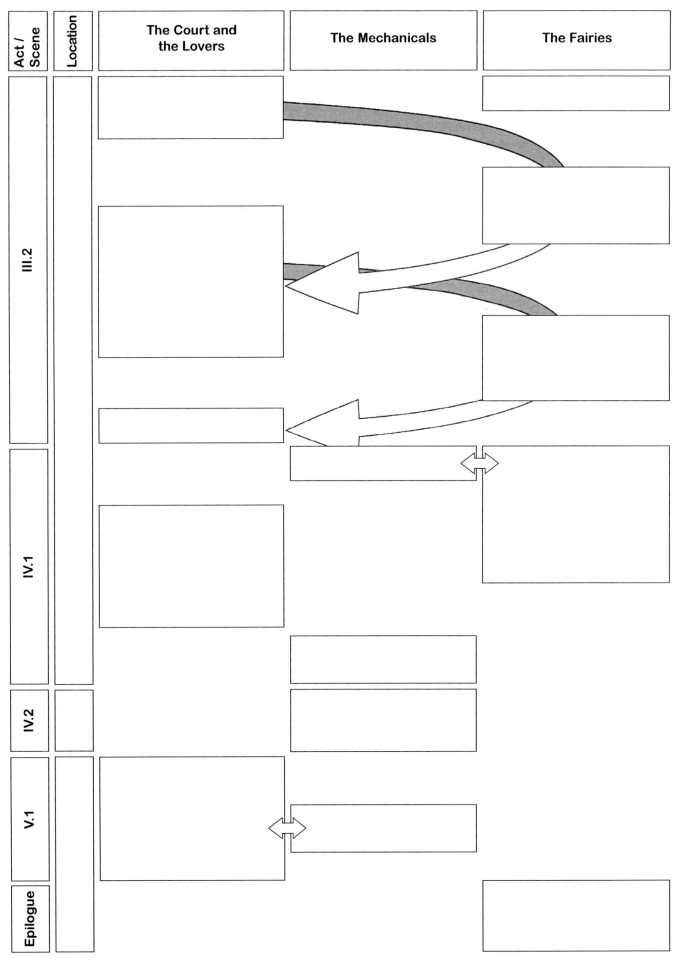

EXPLORING CHARACTER

A Midsummer Night's Dream is an interesting play, as it has no real central or lead character(s). Theseus, for example, although marginal to the main plot-line, has the second largest part in the play when judged by the number of lines spoken (233). Bottom, the character with the largest part, has 261 lines. The other leading characters all have a similar amount of lines: Helena (229), Oberon (226), Puck (209), Lysander (178), Hermia (166), Titania (158), and Demetrius (134).

As a result of this equality of roles, the characters are usually looked at and analyzed in groups: thus there are the lovers, the Athenian court, the fairies, and the Mechanicals. Grouping the characters like this does not suggest those in one group are all the same, but it can help to highlight the differences. Many people, for example, have difficulty telling the lovers apart, just as Puck did. Although this is Shakespeare's intention, there are subtle differences between them.

The Mechanicals provide comic relief in most performances although, as characters, they are sincere. While Bottom is the main role and star here and the others (with the exception of Peter Quince) do not have a lot to say, they are nevertheless all different character types that contribute in their own way to the play.

Titania and Oberon can be seen as mirrors of Hippolyta and Theseus. Their fairy world in the woods poses a threat to the mortals as the fairies interfere with their lives. However, the fairies have their own troubles to sort out, too. While Titania seems to be more passive, Oberon and Puck drive the plot forward and engage themselves actively in complicating life for the lovers.

The Athenian court (Theseus, Hippolyta and Egeus) serves to start the plot-line of the lovers but has no other plot-related function. However, a number of the themes of the play are highlighted in these characters.

THE MAIN CHARACTERS
"Call forth your actors by the scroll"

THE ATHENIAN COURT
Theseus

Theseus is the Duke of Athens and the ruler of all the people we meet in the play. He has had many lovers and conquered many lands. In the play, he recently conquered the Amazons and intends to marry their queen, Hippolyta.

As a ruler, Theseus is law-abiding, though he will try to mitigate the law when he believes it to be too harsh (he converts the death sentence threatening Hermia into eternal isolation). However, he will not have authority questioned and backs Egeus's initial claim. His treatment of the Mechanicals shows him to be fair and magnanimous – he appreciates the effort they have made and the difficulties they have had, as simple workmen, to produce the play.

He seems rational, driven by thought rather than feelings. His speech in V.1 suggests that he looks down upon dreamers and poets, thus denying the emotional side of his character. It is interesting to note that he intends to win Hippolyta over "with pomp, with triumph, and with revelling" (I.1) – there is no talk of love. So, although a great leader and fair judge, it seems his emotional side is lacking.

Hippolyta

Although Hippolyta has a minor role, she seems to have a profound influence on Theseus for the better, becalming him. She has little to say, but Theseus's frequent references to her suggest he is trying to please her. She appears to be quite straightforward in her comments to the Mechanicals' performance of the play, but gentle. She is obviously thrilled by the hunt – a true warrior queen.

Although she echoes Theseus's longing for the moon to change at the end of the play, we never know for sure whether she actually wants to marry Theseus, or perhaps she realizes that, as a captive, she must make the best of a bad situation – hence her silence. If only she would speak more...

THE MAIN CHARACTERS

(cont'd)
Egeus

Egeus's complaint about his daughter Hermia sets off the action in the lovers' plot. Although Lysander and Demetrius are of equal worth and Hermia loves the former, he is intent on marrying his daughter to the latter – even after Demetrius no longer wants Hermia, but Helena again (IV.1). Thus (as we never know why he prefers Demetrius) his wish represents parental arbitrariness in its most extreme form. His wishes are overruled by Theseus; from then on he is silent and we never know what Egeus thinks of the outcome.

THE FAIRIES
Oberon

Like Theseus, Oberon is a ruler who expects absolute obedience. In this respect he is not only jealous, but zealous too. When Titania goes against his bidding he refuses to forgive her until he has punished her. He therefore seems to be yet another male who subdues women.

However, he appears to be genuinely concerned about the fate of mortals and willing to help them in their troubles, as his attempts to ensure the lovers receive their "correct" partner show. It is Helena's futile love of Demetrius that spurs him into action. While his methods (using magic) may be questionable, the result certainly isn't. Thus he can be seen as the archetypal ruler who is not interested in the means, so long as the goal is achieved. As a protector of "damsels in distress" but a harsh husband, he is typically an "old-school" gentleman.

Puck

Puck is one of the most versatile characters in the play. He is jester to Oberon and never far from mischief. When he is introduced to us, the fairy says he will help people who treat him kindly, although we never witness this on stage. He is full of energy and enthusiasm and seems genuinely eager to please Oberon, his master. There is a childish joy rather than malevolence in all his doings, and he relishes the success of his pranks; Puck only seems to want to entertain – even if that is at the expense of others.

Although Puck's mistake in his dealing with the lovers is understandable and seems accidental, the audience cannot help but think that Puck may actually know more than he is letting on, confusing the male lovers on purpose.

Interestingly, it is Puck who solicits the audience's approval in the epilogue, rather than Oberon or another, more powerful figure. As prime origin of mischief, as the one who has been the root of the various misunderstandings and transformations, it is almost as if he is promising the audience that he will better himself.

Titania

Titania shares womanly bonds with her Indian priestess, which makes her want to look after the changeling herself. Although she appears to dominate Oberon in their first encounter, taking control of the altercation, she has to submit to his will, even though this submission is gained through magic rather than persuasion or force of will. Oberon's victory is therefore not complete.

Titania is ridiculed into submission, and she is very much aware of the indignity of her passion for Bottom. She is able to set this aside though, acknowledging Oberon as her lord. This is rather troubling, as her emotions cannot have suddenly been wiped away. She must be aware that Oberon tricked her into giving up the changeling, and so it comes as a surprise that she is willing to forget her previous vehemence and accept Oberon as her lord. Maybe her fairy nature has something to do with this, or maybe she is reconciling for the good of humanity to stop the quarreling. We shall never know.

THE MAIN CHARACTERS

(cont'd)

THE LOVERS

Hermia

Hermia is the smaller of the women, about which she has a slight inferiority complex. She is passionate in her defense of what she believes in and is not afraid to speak out in front of the Duke. She is also prepared to follow Lysander out of Athens so they can marry, displaying great dedication to her lover.

When attacked by Helena, she reacts sharply and seems more willing to let the argument develop into a physical fight. Being loyal herself, she does not understand the changing attachments of the male lovers.

Helena

Helena is tall and fair (at least compared to Hermia). She is similar to Hermia in many ways, possibly to show how the lovers are interchangeable, but also possibly because the two women grew up together.

Helena seems to be more devious and manipulative. When Lysander and Hermia confide in her, she betrays her friend's trust for the chance to indulge her lovesickness. Although she later evokes images of their youth spent in harmony when she believes Hermia to be mocking her, she is the one who first forgets the bands that bind the two women. Also, when Hermia threatens her, Helena seeks the protection of the men, showing her to be more scheming.

Lysander & Demetrius

If the two female lovers are almost indistinguishable, the men are even more so: Lysander even admits that they are of equal standing and riches. The differences are slight, but audiences tend to prefer Lysander to Demetrius. This is because Lysander remains true to Hermia and only switches his object of affection under the influence of the love potion. Demetrius, however,

originally loved Helena but then loves Hermia, even though Lysander loves her and she him. We do not know why Demetrius switched (did Egeus have anything to do with it?). Another fact that makes Demetrius less amiable is the way he treats Helena when she follows him into the woods. He threatens her and we believe he could carry out his threat – a sense of menace we never have with Lysander.

THE MECHANICALS

Bottom

Bottom is convinced of his abilities as an actor. He is enthusiastic to the point of being a nuisance. In the eyes of the other Mechanicals, he is a star who alone can ensure the success of their performance. He strives to use more select language but usually ends up using malapropisms – a sign of someone acting above their station. He can be seen as an annoying know-it-all who is not even scared of lecturing his Duke, and who wants to ensure everyone shares his vision. However, he can also be portrayed more gently, as someone whose only chance to develop himself and escape the squalor of his life is the stage, even though he is no great actor. His childish enthusiasm for escapism sometimes gets the better of him, but there is nothing patronizing about him. Puck's view of him is obviously that he is a pompous ass, which he exemplifies most effectively.

His experience in the woods superficially does not seem to change him, but his speech alone, before he returns to Athens, suggests that some residue remains with him and may yet work upon him. After all, being beloved of the fairy queen cannot leave such a man unaffected.

CHARACTER ACTIVITIES
"I in this affair do thee employ"

Character work can focus either on one group of characters, or on comparing characters from different groups. One important way to explore a character is to see how they react to other people: what they do and say in response to the lines of other characters. Indeed, in a play script, with the exception of any soliloquies, this is the only way to deduce character.

The Lovers
Work here could focus on the constancy of the female lovers, set against the changing affections of the men. Another possible focus is the relationship between Hermia and Helena, which is referred to by both of them as a good and long-lasting friendship, but which, under the strain of the shifting loves of the men, comes under severe pressure.

- The way affections are transferred between the lovers due to the intervention of Puck and the juice of the love-in-idleness flower has often been compared to a dance. There are four distinct stages of this roundel: the opening constellation, two steps between, depending on which male is under the influence of the potion, and then the end constellation, where "Jack has Jill".

- People often notice how similar the lovers are. Indeed, Shakespeare seems to have made the lovers interchangeable on purpose, to show how ridiculous their antics are and how strange love itself is. To explore to what extent the lovers are alike, the pupils can do a "spot-the-difference" exercise that focuses on what the characters share in common, and what separates them. This can be a first step to acting out the characters or to an essay on the lovers.

- Pupils could be asked to write a stream of consciousness piece as either Helena or Hermia in the heat of the conflict of Act III Scene 2. What does she make of the changing affections of the men? Why does she turn against her friend of old? Obviously, the text of the play must be the starting point, but pupils can develop their own thoughts from there.

The Mechanicals
The Mechanicals are the most homogeneous group: they all work together to stage the play, and there is little antagonism between them – save possibly between Bottom and Quince. Bottom, of course, is the main character, but the other Mechanicals are by no means colorless, as their interactions show.

- Taking the rehearsal of the Mechanicals in Act III Scene 1, pupils could analyze what they learn about each laborer from this interaction, also taking their names and professions into account.

- Much of the play's comedy stems from the obvious incapability of the Mechanicals to act their chosen play. Not only do they overact, they often get words wrong and have no sense of the suspension of disbelief that is so vital an ingredient in all theatre. But to what extent are the Mechanicals really bad actors, or mis-cast in their roles? Their view of acting may be wrong, but does that mean they are all wrong in their roles? Using their names, occupations and what we know about them from the play, pupils could explore how each might act and how that fits within the play they intend to perform.

- We learn a lot about Bottom's thoughts and ideas, but what does Peter Quince think of his star? Pupils could write a stream of consciousness piece showing Quince's thoughts about Bottom either after Act I Scene 2 or after Bottom has been "translated" in Act III Scene 2. The only opinions he shares about Bottom appear in Act IV Scene 2.

The Fairies
The most active of the fairies and the one most worth exploring is Robin Goodfellow, or Puck. He is something of a free agent, bringing chaos into the lives of both the lovers and the Mechanicals. His impish nature seems intent on causing mischief – a fun aspect for pupils to explore.

- Pupils can take a close look at Puck's pranks, as described by the fairy and himself at the beginning of Act II Scene 1. Pupils can be asked to visualize them in an illustration and to find common features. Based on these, they can then be asked to invent their own pranks and act them out.

- The fairy king and queen are often regarded as subconscious doubles of Theseus and Hippolyta. Taking this approach as a starting point, pupils could explore to what extent the human dukedom is similar to the fairy kingdom. Of particular interest here is to what extent the fairy court lives out latent desires of the Athenian court.

- Titania reconciles herself very quickly with the fact that Oberon enchanted her to gain the Indian boy in Act IV Scene 1. What might move her to do this is an interesting topic for a stream of consciousness piece in the character of Titania.

The Athenian Court

The Athenian court frames the main plot-line and also starts the action of the lovers. Additionally, it is the background for the plot of the Mechanicals. As characters, Theseus and Hippolyta are not very developed, although the former is certainly more so than the latter. As has been said above, the relationship between Theseus and Hippolyta can be compared to the relationship between Oberon and Titania.

- We never know to what extent Hippolyta loves Theseus. How does she feel about the wedding? Pupils can explore her thoughts and feelings after Act I Scene 1 using stream of consciousness writing.

- Hippolyta's most extended speech is about hounds, while out hunting with Theseus (Act IV Scene 1). Pupils can explore what this tells us about her and her view of her marriage, future husband, and their life together.

- Egeus starts the main complication of the lovers' plot by forbidding his daughter to marry the man she loves. He still insists she marry Demetrius, even after events have turned against him. Theseus overrules him, and he has no further speech in the play. What does he think about events? How might he react to the triple wedding? Pupils can explore this using stream of consciousness or by examining his character based on what he says in the play.

Character Sheets

There are a number of questions or issues that are central to each character. These can be given to the pupils in the form of a worksheet. Pupils should start on different questions and then be asked to work clockwise around the worksheet. After a set time, pupils can work in groups to compare the worksheets, and fill in any missing information or sections. This resource provides character sheets for Bottom, Oberon, Puck, Titania, Helena and Theseus.

Blank Comic Sheets

Pivotal moments of the play can also be used to explore emotions (and thus character) using blank comic pages (page 35). Instead of filling in what the characters are saying (Shakespeare tells us this already), pupils can be asked to fill in what the characters are thinking, using thought bubbles and conforming to comic book layout rules (e.g. order of reading from top left to bottom right, bold writing to emphasize words in the text). The drawing can be rudimentary "stick-men" – anything as long as some essence of mood and/or story is captured.

Venn Diagrams

Venn diagrams are used in logic and mathematics to show what various sets have in common. This technique can also be used to explore the similarities and differences (which can be as simple or complex as the pupils like) of any three characters.

One way to use Venn diagrams is to split the class into groups and give each group a different set of three characters to analyze. Using a template or anything circular, the Venn diagrams should be drawn on large paper or card. Each group should be given some time to fill in its diagram. Afterwards, each group moves so that they are in front of the Venn diagram of a different group. Give them some time to look at this diagram and to make comments on it. The comments can then be discussed and resolved in class.

BOTTOM CHARACTER SHEET

Do you think Bottom is happy with his lot in life?

Is Bottom too domineering?

Is Bottom a good actor?

In what way might the time with Titania have changed Bottom?

PUCK CHARACTER SHEET

Why does Puck play his pranks?

How does Puck see his Queen, Titania?

Does Puck like Oberon?

What age do you think Puck is? In what way might Puck's age influence our view of him?

OBERON CHARACTER SHEET

Is Oberon a just ruler of fairyland?

Do you think Oberon thinks only of himself?

Why does Oberon want the changeling boy so much?

Why does Oberon help the lovers?

TITANIA CHARACTER SHEET

Is Titania right to withhold the changeling boy from Oberon?

Why do you think Titania sleeps so often?

What kind of a ruler is Titania?

Why does Titania give in to Oberon so easily?

HELENA CHARACTER SHEET

How does Helena feel about loving Demetrius?

Do you think Helena would really want to be Hermia?

Why does Helena think that everyone is mocking her?

What makes Helena change her mind and believe Demetrius loves her?

THESEUS CHARACTER SHEET

Will Theseus manage to get Hippolyta to love him?

Is Theseus a good Duke?

Is Theseus fair in overruling Egeus?

In what way do you think Hippolyta influences Theseus?

VENN DIAGRAMS

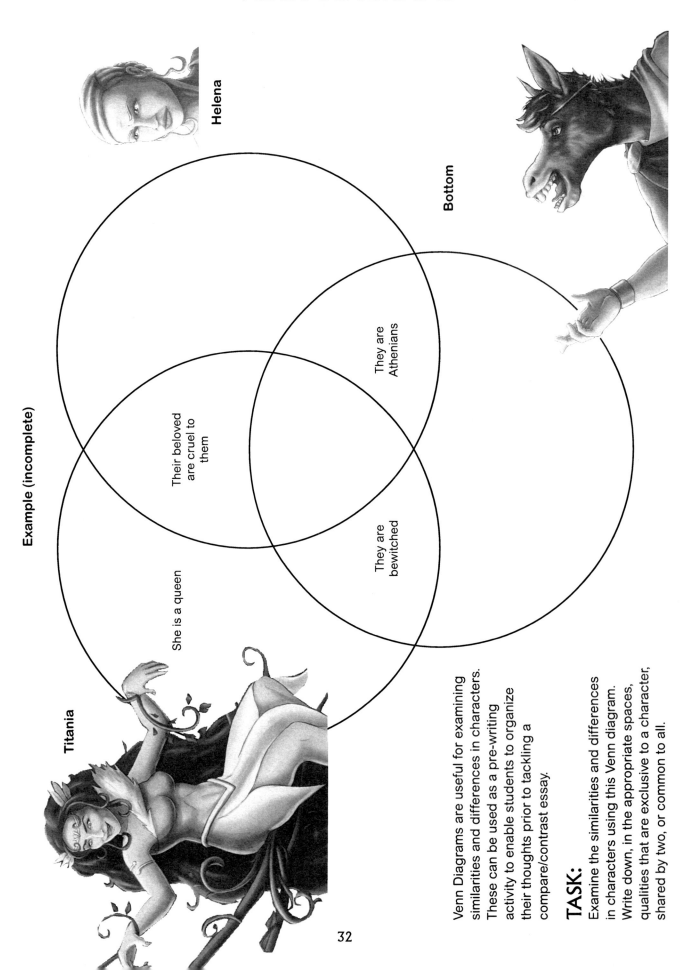

Helena

Bottom

Example (incomplete)

They are
Athenians

Their beloved
are cruel to
them

They are
bewitched

She is a queen

Titania

Venn Diagrams are useful for examining
similarities and differences in characters.
These can be used as a pre-writing
activity to enable students to organize
their thoughts prior to tackling a
compare/contrast essay.

TASK:

Examine the similarities and differences
in characters using this Venn diagram.
Write down, in the appropriate spaces,
qualities that are exclusive to a character,
shared by two, or common to all.

32

VENN DIAGRAMS

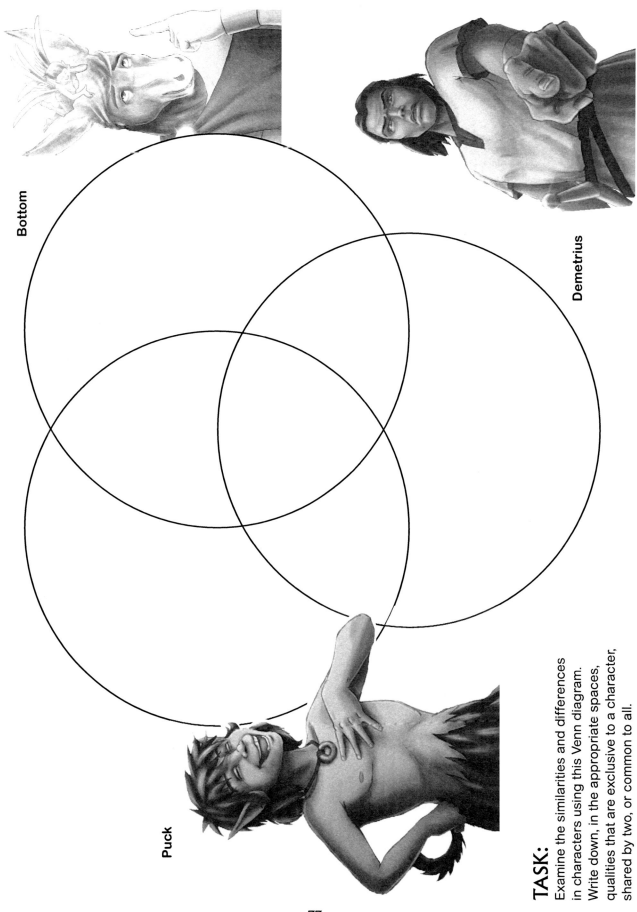

Bottom

Demetrius

Puck

TASK:
Examine the similarities and differences in characters using this Venn diagram. Write down, in the appropriate spaces, qualities that are exclusive to a character, shared by two, or common to all.

VENN DIAGRAMS

Oberon

Hermia

Theseus

TASK:

Examine the similarities and differences in characters using this Venn diagram. Write down, in the appropriate spaces, qualities that are exclusive to a character, shared by two, or common to all.

BLANK COMIC GRID

SPOT THE DIFFERENCE
"I am, my lord, well deriv'd as he, as well possess'd"

TASK:
Use the following charts to explore to what extent the lovers are similar and different. For the men you might want to differentiate between when they are under the influence of the love juice and when they are not (particularly for Lysander). Compare the number of differences between the men and the number between the women. What does this say about Shakespeare's portrayal of each gender?

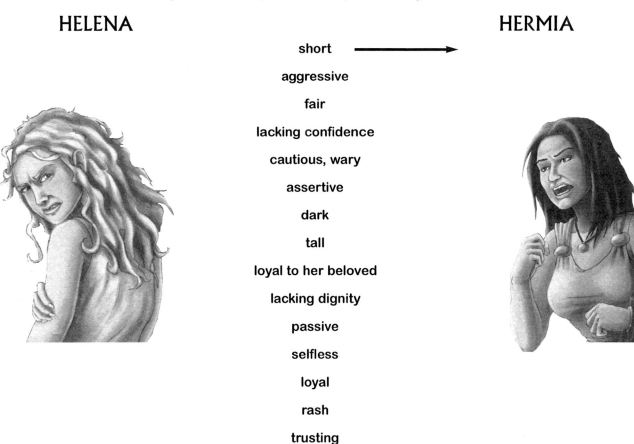

HELENA   **HERMIA**

short   ⟶

aggressive

fair

lacking confidence

cautious, wary

assertive

dark

tall

loyal to her beloved

lacking dignity

passive

selfless

loyal

rash

trusting

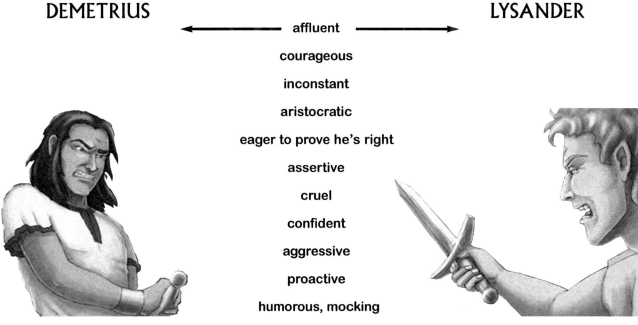

DEMETRIUS   **LYSANDER**

⟵   affluent   ⟶

courageous

inconstant

aristocratic

eager to prove he's right

assertive

cruel

confident

aggressive

proactive

humorous, mocking

DUKEDOM AND KINGDOM
"Come, my queen, take hands with me"

In many modern productions of the play, as they never appear on stage at the same time, the roles of Titania and Oberon are doubled up with Hippolyta and Theseus, respectively – meaning one actor plays both Oberon and Theseus, while another plays both Titania and Hippolyta. In what way does the fairy court mirror the Athenian court? Use this sheet to help you explore the issue.

	The Athenian Court	The Fairy Court
What is the relationship between the rulers like?		
What problem(s) do they have?		
How does Theseus / Oberon intend to solve the problem(s)		
How are Theseus / Oberon's spirits lifted?		
How do they behave toward their subjects?		
What might the Athenian Court learn from the Fairy Court?		
What might the Fairy Court learn from the Athenian Court?		

THE MECHANICALS REHEARSE
(from Act III Scene 1)

BOTTOM
Are we all met?

QUINCE
Pat, pat; and here's a marvellous convenient place for our rehearsal. This green plot shall be our stage, this hawthorn-brake our tiring-house; and we will do it in action as we will do it before the duke.

BOTTOM
Peter Quince,--

QUINCE
What sayest thou, bully Bottom?

BOTTOM
There are things in this comedy of "Pyramus and Thisbe" that will never please. First, Pyramus must draw a sword to kill himself; which the ladies cannot abide. How answer you that?

SNOUT
By'r lakin, a parlous fear.

STARVELING
I believe we must leave the killing out, when all is done.

BOTTOM
Not a whit: I have a device to make all well. Write me a prologue; and let the prologue seem to say, we will do no harm with our swords, and that Pyramus is not killed indeed; and, for the more better assurance, tell them that I, Pyramus, am not Pyramus, but Bottom the weaver: this will put them out of fear.

QUINCE
Well, we will have such a prologue; and it shall be written in eight and six.

BOTTOM
No, make it two more; let it be written in eight and eight.

SNOUT
Will not the ladies be afeard of the lion?

STARVELING
I fear it, I promise you.

BOTTOM
Masters, you ought to consider with yourselves: to bring in – God shield us! – a lion among ladies, is a most dreadful thing; for there is not a more fearful wild-fowl than your lion living, and we ought to look to it.

In what way are both Bottom and Quince trying to take charge?

Why do you think Bottom might be trying to test Quince?

With whom do the others side and why?

If Bottom has a solution, why did he mention it as a problem above?

How would they say this? Are Bottom and Quince fighting or is Bottom just correcting Quince?

What does this line suggest about Snout?

Surely Bottom knows they won't bring on a real lion. So why is he saying this?

SNOUT

Therefore, another prologue must tell he is not a lion.

BOTTOM

Nay, you must name his name, and half his face must be seen through the lion's neck; and he himself must speak through, saying thus, or to the same defect,– "Ladies,"– or, "Fair ladies, I would wish you," – or, "I would request you,"– or, "I would entreat you, not to fear, not to tremble: my life for yours. If you think I come hither as a lion, it were pity of my life: no, I am no such thing; I am a man as other men are;" and there, indeed, let him name his name, and tell them plainly, he is Snug the joiner.

QUINCE

Well it shall be so. But there is two hard things: that is, to bring the moonlight into a chamber; for, you know, Pyramus and Thisbe meet by moonlight.

SNOUT

Doth the moon shine that night we play our play?

BOTTOM

A calendar, a calendar! look in the almanac; find out moonshine, find out moonshine.

QUINCE

Yes, it doth shine that night.

BOTTOM

Why, then may you leave a casement of the great chamber-window, where we play, open; and the moon may shine in at the casement.

QUINCE

Ay; or else one must come in with a bush of thorns and a lantern, and say he comes to disfigure, or to present, the person of Moonshine. Then, there is another thing: we must have a wall in the great chamber; for Pyramus and Thisbe says the story, did talk through the chink of a wall.

SNOUT

You can never bring in a wall. What say you, Bottom?

BOTTOM

Some man or other must present Wall: and let him have some plaster, or some loam, or some rough-cast about him, to signify wall; and let him hold his fingers thus, and through that cranny shall Pyramus and Thisbe whisper.

QUINCE

If that may be, then all is well. Come, sit down, every mother's son, and rehearse your parts. Pyramus, you begin. When you have spoken your speech, enter into that brake; and so every one according to his cue.

Why does Bottom not agree with Snout?

Why does Quince highlight these problems?

Does Snout want to be like Bottom?

Why does Quince say "Ay" when he then disagrees with Bottom?

Why does Snout ask Bottom rather than Quince, the director?

Why does Bottom copy the idea Quince had for the moon?

39

HIPPOLYTA THE HUNTRESS
"The bouncing Amazon, your buskin'd mistress and your warrior love"

Hippolyta's longest speech is in Act IV Scene 1 when she talks about hunting hounds. Theseus has just praised his own hounds, and she responds as below. What does this speech tell us about Hippolyta?

Theseus has just mentioned his hounds – why does she mention these (possibly more famous) hounds here?

Why does Hippolyta mention two such outstanding heroes in front of Theseus?

I was with Hercules* and Cadmus* once,

When in a wood of Crete they bay'd the bear

With hounds of Sparta*: never did I hear

Such gallant chiding; for, besides the groves,

The skies, the fountains, every region near

Seem'd all one mutual cry. I never heard

So musical a discord, such sweet thunder.

She calls the barking of the hounds "sweet thunder". What does this tell us about her?

Twice Hippolyta says she "never" heard such noise. What does this suggest?

Hercules: a mythological hero who was the strongest man alive
Cadmus: another mythological figure; the founder of Thebes
Sparta: a region in Greece renowned for its warriors and hunting hounds

EGEUS – THE LUCKLESS FATHER
"I beg the law, the law, upon his head"

Act I Scene 1

Full of vexation come I, with complaint
Against my child, my daughter Hermia.
Stand forth, Demetrius. My noble lord,
This man hath my consent to marry her.
Stand forth, Lysander; and, my gracious duke,
This man hath bewitch'd the bosom of my child;
[...]
With cunning hast thou filch'd my daughter's heart,
Turn'd her obedience, which is due to me,
To stubborn harshness. And, my gracious duke,
Be it so she will not here before your grace
Consent to marry with Demetrius,
I beg the ancient privilege of Athens:
As she is mine, I may dispose of her;
Which shall be either to this gentleman,
Or to her death, according to our law
Immediately provided in that case.

> What kind of a father is Egeus? Is his point of view right? Are his directives fair? practical? reasonable?

Act IV Scene 1
EGEUS

Enough, enough! my lord, you have enough.
I beg the law, the law, upon his head.
They would have stol'n away; they would, Demetrius,
Thereby to have defeated you and me;
You of your wife, and me of my consent,
Of my consent that she should be your wife.
[...]

> Is Egeus being sensible here, considering the situation?

THESEUS

Egeus, I will overbear your will;
For in the temple, by and by, with us
These couples shall eternally be knit;

> How might Egeus react to this?

SHAKESPEARE'S LANGUAGE

Introduction

Apart from Shakespeare's wide and diverse vocabulary and somewhat unusual diction or word order, the two main issues that pupils find difficult with Shakespeare are the prosody (verse structure) of his writing and the imagery.

The vocabulary issue can only be tackled with a glossary or dictionary, although some knowledge of foreign languages (especially French and Latin) may help. The difficulty students have with the word order is more baffling, especially as most pupils have no difficulty comprehending what Yoda (of *Star Wars* fame) says. Patience the answer here must be.

Prosody:

In *A Midsummer Night's Dream*, Shakespeare uses a variety of different verse forms to bring out the character of the various groups. Thus the Athenian court usually speaks in blank verse, the lovers in rhymed couplets, and the Mechanicals in prose (Shakespeare often used prose/verse and rhyme to denote class). Although prosody can be technically difficult, it is worthwhile for the pupils to examine the effect of the different kinds of verse form, using the number of stresses per line to guide them. Before examining the various types of verse used in the play, pupils should be confident with identifying iambic pentameter – Shakespeare's predominant meter.

A line of iambic pentameter contains five iambs. An iamb consists of two syllables, the first one being unstressed, the second stressed (ti-TUM). So the basic line of Shakespearean poetry has ten syllables with every second syllable stressed as follows (each "x" representing a syllable):

e.g.,

x	>X<	x	>X<	x	>X<	x	>X<	x	>X<

Lines of iambic pentameter that don't rhyme are called blank verse.

Now,	fair	Hi-	ppol-	y-	ta,	our	nup-	tial	hour

Also, Shakespeare's lines aren't always pure iambic pentameter; there are sometimes extra, unstressed syllables added in.

Some ideas for work on the structure of Shakespeare's language:

- To discover the rhythm of Shakespeare's lines, the pupils can practice splitting the lines up into syllables and then discovering where the stresses are, using pure iambic pentameter as a guideline. Once they have understood the concept, they can write a few lines of their own in iambic pentameter.

- Pupils could be asked to analyze typical speech for each group and try to explain the effect achieved by using different types of verse forms. Pupils should look at rhythm, rhyme, and word choice.

- After having examined various styles of versification, pupils could write their own short verse speech, using a style befitting their chosen character.

- Another frequent problem pupils have with verse is that they tend to read it to the end of a line rather than from punctuation mark to punctuation mark. Peter Quince's prologue is an excellent example of how lines of verse can be misread by stopping in the wrong place.

SHAKESPEARE'S LANGUAGE

Imagery:

Some of the beauty of Shakespeare's language (as well as its difficulty) stems from his daring and original use of imagery. The main techniques used are similes and metaphors. It is important to bear in mind that both are images, and both are comparisons that derive their effectiveness and strength from the degree to which the first element is similar to the second. The more effective the image, the more levels it will work on, and also the more it will challenge received opinion or cliché.

Some ideas for work on language are:

- Examine some stylistic elements that are either typically Shakespearean (like antithesis) or peculiar to a character like Bottom's malapropisms.

- Use one of Shakespeare's more descriptive passages to kick-start a descriptive piece, if possible using some of Shakespeare's techniques.

- After pupils have discovered the main features of a character's speech, they could try their own hand at writing some dialogue for that character, staying true to their personality. This could also be in iambic pentameter if this has already been discussed, to provide a real challenge.

- For more focused work on imagery, pupils can be asked to search for a number of similes and metaphors and explain their effect, first analyzing what the second element means, and then how this relates to the first element. This should be a good starting point to then explain why the image is effective or why/how it fails.

- Shakespeare is also famous for his unusual and inventive insults. *A Midsummer Night's Dream* contains a small helping of these, mainly when the lovers are at loggerheads. For a more fun activity, pupils can search these out (in III.2) and then hurl them at each other, using different tones of voice (menacing, mocking, sarcastic, hurt, etc.).

THE RHYTHM OF SHAKESPEARE'S LANGUAGE
"It is not enough to speak, but to speak true"

Use the grid below to help you highlight the iambic pentameter in the following lines of Theseus's speech in Act V Scene 1. The basic rhythm for this is written down at the top of the table. Each syllable should occupy one box. Remember that not every line has to be pure iambic pentameter, and some word groups can be pronounced as one or two syllables (such as "poet").

> The lunatic, the lover, and the poet,
> Are of imagination all compact:
> One sees more devils than vast hell can hold;
> That is the madman: the lover, all as frantic,
> Sees Helen's beauty in a brow of Egypt:
> The poet's eye, in a fine frenzy rolling,
> Doth glance from heaven to earth, from earth to heaven;
> And as imagination bodies forth
> The forms of things unknown, the poet's pen
> Turns them to shapes, and gives to airy nothing
> A local habitation, and a name.

X The	>X< lun-	X a-	>X< tic,	X the	>X< lov-	X er,	>X< and	X the	>X< poet,		

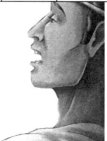

QUINCE SPEAKS THE PROLOGUE
"This fellow doth not stand upon points"

Quince, in his nervousness, mixes up the punctuation of his prologue in front of the Duke. Printed below is the piece as he delivers it, as well as the same prologue without punctuation. See if you can work out where the punctuation should belong.

Prologue
If we offend, it is with our good will.
That you should think, we come not to offend,
But with good will. To show our simple skill,
That is the true beginning of our end.
Consider then, we come but in despite.
We do not come as minding to content you,
Our true intent is. All for your delight
We are not here. That you should here repent you,
The actors are at hand; and, by their show,
You shall know all, that you are like to know.

TASK:
Punctuate this correctly:

if we offend it is with our good will

that you should think we come not to offend

but with good will to show our simple skill

that is the true beginning of our end

consider then we come but in despite

we do not come as minding to content you

our true intent is all for your delight

we are not here that you should here repent you

the actors are at hand and by their show

you shall know all that you are like to know

THE GROUPS AND THEIR LANGUAGE
"Tongue-tied simplicity in least speak most"

First of all determine the rhyme and rhythm (if applicable) of each group's speech, and then explain what effect this has on how the characters in the group are perceived.

The character's words	What does the poetic form tell us about the character?
ATHENIAN COURT	
THESEUS (talking to Hippolyta in Act I Scene 1) Now, fair Hippolyta, our nuptial hour Draws on apace: four happy days bring in Another moon; but, O, methinks, how slow This old moon wanes! she lingers my desires, Like to a step-dame, or a dowager, Long withering out a young man's revenue.	What can you say about the rhythm and rhyme? What effect does this mode of speaking have?
FAIRIES	
TITANIA (rebuking Oberon in Act II Scene 1) And never, since the middle summer's spring, Met we on hill, in dale, forest or mead, By paved fountain or by rushy brook, Or in the beached margent of the sea, To dance our ringlets to the whistling wind, But with thy brawls thou hast disturb'd our sport.	What can you say about the rhythm and rhyme? What effect does this mode of speaking have?
TITANIA (talking to her fairies in Act III Scene 1) Come, wait upon him; lead him to my bower. The moon, methinks, looks with a watery eye; And when she weeps, weeps every little flower, Lamenting some enforced chastity. Tie up my love's tongue, bring him silently.	What can you say about the rhythm and rhyme? What effect does this mode of speaking have?

THE GROUPS AND THEIR LANGUAGE

(cont'd)

The character's words	What does the poetic form tell us about the character?
PUCK (alone in Act II Scene 2) Through the forest have I gone, But Athenian found I none, On whose eyes I might approve This flower's force in stirring love. Night and silence – who is here? Weeds of Athens he doth wear: This is he, my master said, Despised the Athenian maid; And here the maiden, sleeping sound, On the dank and dirty ground.	What can you say about the rhythm and rhyme? What effect does this mode of speaking have?
PUCK (talking to Oberon in Act III Scene 2) Near to her close and consecrated bower, While she was in her dull and sleeping hour, A crew of patches, rude Mechanicals, That work for bread upon Athenian stalls, Were met together to rehearse a play, Intended for great Theseus' nuptial day.	What can you say about the rhythm and rhyme? What effect does this mode of speaking have?
MECHANICALS	
PETER QUINCE (talking to the Mechanicals in Act I Scene 2) Here is the scroll of every man's name, which is thought fit, through all Athens, to play in our interlude before the duke and the duchess, on his wedding-day at night.	What can you say about the rhythm and rhyme? What effect does this mode of speaking have?

THE GROUPS AND THEIR LANGUAGE

(cont'd)

The character's words	What does the poetic form tell us about the character?
BOTTOM (as Pyramus in the play, Act V Scene 1) But stay, O spite! But mark, poor knight, What dreadful dole is here? Eyes, do you see? How can it be? O dainty duck! O dear! Thy mantle good, What! stain'd with blood? Approach, ye Furies fell! O Fates, come, come; Cut thread and thrum; Quail, crush, conclude, and quell!	What can you say about the rhythm and rhyme? What effect does this mode of speaking have?
LOVERS	
HERMIA (talking to Lysander in Act I Scene 1) I swear to thee, by Cupid's strongest bow, By his best arrow with the golden head, By the simplicity of Venus' doves, By that which knitteth souls and prospers loves, And by that fire which burn'd the Carthage queen, When the false Trojan under sail was seen, By all the vows that ever men have broke, In number more than ever women spoke: In that same place thou hast appointed me, To-morrow truly will I meet with thee.	What can you say about the rhythm and rhyme? What effect does this mode of speaking have?

ANTITHESIS
"Merry and tragical? Tedious and brief?"

One of Shakespeare's favorite figures of speech is antithesis – putting opposites next to each other. There are a number of instances of this in *A Midsummer Night's Dream*. For example in Act III Scene 2, Lysander says to Demetrius,

Thou canst compel no more than she entreat:

Thy threats have no more strength than her weak prayers.

"compel" (force) and "entreat" (beg) are opposites, as are "strength" and "weak," but "threats" and "prayers" are also opposites.

TASK:

Now explore the opposites in these two short extracts from Act I Scene 1. Each underlined word has an opposite – find the opposite from the words at the bottom and fill it in the correct place of the speech (without referring to the play)

LYSANDER
>   The course of true love never did run smooth;
>   But, either it was different in blood,--

HERMIA
>   O cross! too _____ to be enthrall'd to low!

LYSANDER
>   Or else misgraffed in respect of years,--

HERMIA
>   O spite! too _____ to be engag'd to young!

HELENA
>   O, that your _____ would teach my smiles such skill!

HERMIA
>   I give him curses, yet he gives me _____ .

HELENA
>   O, that my prayers could such affection move!

HERMIA
>   The more I _____ , the more he follows me.

HELENA
>   The more I _____ , the more he hateth me.

love   hate   high   old   love   frowns

49

BOTTOM'S "BOTTOMISMS"
"There is not one word apt"

Part of the comedy the Mechanicals offer in *A Midsummer Night's Dream* is that they are trying to act a "lofty" (as Bottom would call it) play, but they are themselves rough and ready laborers without a broad vocabulary – which doesn't mean they don't try! Unfortunately for them, and fortunately for the audience, they are not usually successful; and often they, and in particular Bottom, use malapropisms: wrong words that sound similar to the words that should be used.

TASK:

Use the following grid to explore what word the Mechanical wants to say, and what the word he uses actually means.

	What word should he have used?	What does the word he has used mean?
You were best to call them generally, man by man (I.2)		
but I will aggravate my voice so, that I will roar you as gently as any sucking dove (I.2)		
and there we may rehearse, most obscenely and courageously (I.2)		
he himself must speak through, saying thus, or to the same defect, (III.1)		
or else one must [...] and say, he comes to disfigure, or to present, the person of Moonshine (III.1 – Quince)		
I have an exposition of sleep come upon me (IV.1)		
Since lion vile hath here deflower'd my dear (V.1)		

Based on your findings, you might now like to consider in what way malapropisms are funny.

IMAGERY IN *A MIDSUMMER NIGHT'S DREAM*
"His speech was like a tangled chain"

Shakespeare often uses similes (comparisons using "like" or "as [attribute] as a [something]") and metaphors (images) to convey his message and to make his language more effective and interesting. Both techniques rely on the two elements of the image having something in common.

For example: "His speech was like a tangled chain" (simile), where the effectiveness of the simile depends on the "speech" being similar to a "tangled chain". This can be displayed using a Venn diagram:

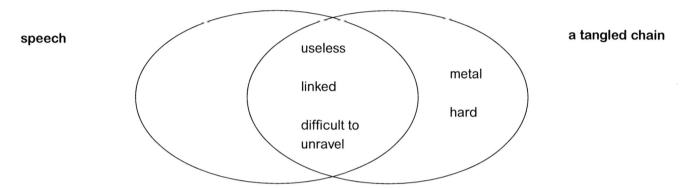

As can be seen, "speech" (depending on what kind of speech it is; here it refers to Quince's mixed up prologue) can be like a "tangled chain". It is linked, because the words work together to make sense, but if spoken incorrectly they become difficult to unravel and no longer make sense, making them useless. Good images (as with this image), be they similes or metaphors, will usually have a number of things in common and also provide some new and startling insight into the object being described.

TASK:

Now that you know how imagery works, try it out for yourself and analyze the imagery Shakespeare uses in *A Midsummer Night's Dream*. Go through the play and find instances of imagery. There are plenty of them to choose from. Use the framework below for your analysis.

Image: _____

Is it a simile or a metaphor?

first element   **second element**

_____   _____

_____

_____

_____

IMAGERY IN *A MIDSUMMER NIGHT'S DREAM*

"Lysander riddles very prettily"

Now that you know how imagery works, try it out for yourself and analyse the imagery Shakespeare uses in *A Midsummer Night's Dream*. Go through the play and find instances of imagery. There are plenty of them to choose from. Use the framework below for your analysis.

Image: _____

Is it a simile or a metaphor?

first element   **second element**

_____   _____

_____

_____

_____

_____

Image: _____

Is it a simile or a metaphor?

first element   **second element**

_____   _____

_____

_____

_____

THE LOVERS' (AND OTHERS') INSULTS
"Curs'd be thy stones for thus deceiving me!"

Use the following grid to jot down the insults the lovers exchange in Act III Scene 2. Can you find any other insults in the play?

Once you have collected a number of insults, you can try them out in pairs – but rather than just shout the insults at each other, try to be in character. How would Hermia and Helena say their insults to each other? How Lysander to Hermia?

Hermia vs. Demetrius

Lysander vs. Hermia

Hermia vs. Helena

Helena vs. Hermia

Demetrius vs. Lysander

Use this grid to jot down any other insults you come across in *A Midsummer Night's Dream*.

Who is insulting whom?	The insult

EXPLORING THEMES IN
A MIDSUMMER NIGHT'S DREAM

Introduction

This chapter focuses on the main themes of *A Midsummer Night's Dream*.
They are (in order of presentation):

- Love and Marriage
- Obedience
- Dreams and Imagination
- The Moon – madness and chastity

There are, of course, areas where these overlap: work on marriage will also have to examine issues of obedience, as one of the marital conflicts presented in the play (between Titania and Oberon) revolves around their disobedience to each other. Similarly, the moon pervades all themes – but in particular the theme of dreams and imagination. These similarities are invitations to explore the themes and their interconnections further. Some themes also interlink with character work – once again, this is an invitation to work broadly and approach one topic from a number of different angles.
At the end of the chapter is a general section that focuses primarily on writing an analytical essay involving one of the themes presented.

SETTING THE THEMES

The beginning of a play – much like the beginning of any story, novel or film – has to fulfill a number of functions. First and foremost it must, of course, grab the attention of the audience. Usually, the main characters are presented at the beginning, or at least near the beginning. Main themes are also habitually introduced in the opening scene.
With its three different groups of characters who inhabit three different worlds, *A Midsummer Night's Dream* obviously cannot present all of the main characters in its opening scene – in fact it only presents one group of characters: the Athenian court. However, it does introduce a number of the main themes that will concern all the groups: the theme of love and marriage, which is equally a theme of the fairy realm (with Oberon and Titania's quarrel) and of the Mechanicals (through their play of *Pyramus and Thisbe*).
A number of themes are listed in the grid opposite. Pupils should be asked to find evidence of these themes in the opening scene of the play. Two rows have been left blank to enable pupils to note down their own ideas and thus take more control of their learning. It is suggested that pupils work in pairs or groups for this activity.

EXPLORING ACT 1 SCENE 1

TASK:

Use the following table to explore to what extent the themes of *A Midsummer Night's Dream*, listed on the left of the page, are present in the opening scene of the play. Remember to back up your thoughts with evidence from the play, and to explain in what way the quotation you have selected involves the theme.

Themes	Evidence from the text	Explain relevance of evidence
Love & Marriage		
Obedience		
Dreams		
Imagination (the mind's eye)		

LOVE AND MARRIAGE

"Reason and love keep little company together now-a-days"

A Midsummer Night's Dream is, above all, a play about love and marriage. Throughout the play, love is the dominant theme and the driving force, and it is highlighted in its various aspects, from adolescent folly to more mature conjugal love.

We are introduced to the theme of marriage in the opening lines of the play – but to what extent this marriage is backed by love, we can never really discern. Hippolyta seems to be freedom-loving, and from Theseus's words, it appears that she does not necessarily love him (although he expresses a desire to win her heart). Despite that, he does seem to feel love for her; beyond that, all else is conjecture. What we do know is that the marriage is a state affair, possibly with the intention of knitting together the recently conquered Amazons with Theseus's realm. Hippolyta seems to accept this state of affairs and is prepared to make the best of the situation.

The other "mature" couple of the play is very different. Titania and Oberon have obviously been together for quite some time. We see them at odds with each other over the issue of the changeling boy; however, they are quick to point out their shortfalls prior to that catalyst. From the events prior to the play and recounted in the text, it seems they did not have the best of relationships; and this current quarrel is having repercussions in nature, affecting the whole world. It is obvious that Oberon desires Titania – how he speaks of her is laden with voluptuousness, and his revenge is equally corporeal. It seems that physicality is a key ingredient to their relationship.

The lovers represent young love, which is portrayed as a mixture of intense emotions, besottedness, of being "in love," and changing one's emotional attachments. There is a lot of dynamic in this youthful love, a reflection of the fact that theirs is an age when people test each other's emotions and commitment prior to marriage. The women stay true to their loves throughout: Helena never ceases loving Demetrius, and Hermia never loves anybody but Lysander. In addition, Hermia at no point believes that Lysander would willingly or knowingly betray her love.

A distinction often made in the play is between doting and loving. The former is a strong but superficial and usually transient passion, not open to reflection or reason, while the latter is a more mature feeling based on an intimate knowledge of the partner's character.

Mixed into this cocktail of lovers and various forms of love is the story of *Pyramus and Thisbe*, a tragic story of love that is reminiscent of *Romeo and Juliet* (which Shakespeare was writing at the same time as *A Midsummer Night's Dream*). *Pyramus and Thisbe* shows how the plot of the play – lovers forbidden to stay together – could have developed, if not for the crazy happenings in the wood.

Some ideas for activities:

- At the end all the couples are (happily) married. To what extent do the pupils think they will live "happily ever after"? Students can use the text as a basis for exploration. For one, Demetrius is never officially cured from the effect of the flower juice. Maybe that is something that will wear off?

- To discover the difference between doting and loving, pupils can compare Lysander's words when he is in love with Hermia with when he is under the influence of the love juice.

- A lot of the confusion of the lovers is due to love-in-idleness. Pupils could write a poem about what is in the juice of that flower, making sure the poem is metaphorical (saying what induces the "doting").

- Pupils could write a stream of consciousness piece in the character of either Lysander or Demetrius about waking up under the influence of the love potion.

- One aspect of love explored in the play is its relationship to reason. Those under the influence of the love potion try to explain their change of heart in different ways. Pupils could explore these passages and draw conclusions on what extent love and reason do or do not mix.

- Compare the main plot elements of the lovers' plot in *A Midsummer Night's Dream*, *Pyramus and Thisbe* and *Romeo and Juliet*. The idea here is to not only see how the plots are similar, but also to discover how similar starting positions can lead to a tragic outcome just as easily as a happy one. How does this realization reflect on our notions of the possibility of a happy ending?

HAPPY EVER AFTER?
"All shall be well"

Use the grid below to explore to what extent you think the couples – all married off or reconciled at the end of the play – will have a happy marriage. Use evidence from the play to support your points.

Couple	Will they live on happily?	Evidence from the text
Theseus & Hippolyta		
Lysander & Hermia		
Demetrius & Helena		
Oberon & Titania		

LYSANDER LOVES AND DOTES
"By all the vows that ever men have broke"

Lysander's true love to Hermia is converted by the love potion into doting on Helena. In what way does this affect his language? Use the grid below to help you explore the difference between loving and doting.

Lysander loves Hermia	Lysander dotes on Helena
How does he address each woman?	
Comparison:	
What imagery does he use? What for?	
Comparison:	
Are there any differences in emotion? Explain how you can tell.	

LOVE AND REASON
"Reason becomes the marshal to my will"

In the course of the play, a number of characters fall unexpectedly in love with others thanks to the workings of love-in-idleness. The reactions of the bewitched to their change of heart is often to try to rationalize the sudden shift in their emotions. Examining their arguments and reactions is a good way to explore the theme of love, and also to find out whether love and reason are irreconcilable, as Bottom suggests.

Titania I pray thee, gentle mortal, sing again: Mine ear is much enamour'd of thy note; So is mine eye enthralled to thy shape; And thy fair virtue's force, perforce, doth move me, On the first view to say, to swear, I love thee. **Bottom** Methinks, mistress, you should have little reason for that: and yet, to say the truth, reason and love keep little company together now-a-days; the more the pity, that some honest neighbours will not make them friends. Nay, I can gleek upon occasion.	What characteristics of Bottom does Titania say she is in love with?
	What tells us that she realizes he is not quite a fit companion?
Titania Thou art as wise as thou art beautiful. **Bottom** Not so, neither: but if I had wit enough to get out of this wood, I have enough to serve mine own turn. **Titania** Out of this wood do not desire to go: Thou shalt remain here, whether thou wilt or no. I am a spirit of no common rate: The summer still doth tend upon my state; And I do love thee: therefore, go with me; I'll give thee fairies to attend on thee; […] And I will purge thy mortal grossness so, That thou shalt like an airy spirit go.	How do we know Titania – though besotted – is still a powerful queen, not to be crossed?
	Why is Titania's love unreasonable?

LOVE AND REASON

(cont'd)

Lysander The will of man is by his reason sway'd, And reason says you are the worthier maid. Things growing are not ripe until their season: So I, being young, till now ripe not to reason; And touching now the point of human skill, Reason becomes the marshal to my will, And leads me to your eyes; where I o'erlook Love's stories, written in love's richest book.	How does Lysander explain his change of feelings? Why do you think he uses reason as an argument? What could you say against this argument?
Demetrius But, my good lord, I wot not by what power,– But by some power it is,– my love to Hermia, Melted as the snow, seems to me now As the remembrance of an idle gaud, Which in my childhood I did dote upon; And all the faith, the virtue of my heart, The object and the pleasure of mine eye, Is only Helena. To her, my lord, Was I betroth'd ere I saw Hermia: But, like a sickness, did I loathe this food; But, as in health, come to my natural taste, Now I do wish it, love it, long for it, And will for evermore be true to it.	How does Demetrius explain that he loves Helena once again? Why is the image of "sickness" particularly apt? What could you say against his argument?

STAR-CROSSED LOVERS
"The course of true love never did run smooth"

In Act I Scene 1, Lysander and Hermia bewail their fate – to love one another, but to have Hermia's father against that union. This set-up is reminiscent of *Pyramus and Thisbe*, which the Mechanicals perform in Act V, and *Romeo and Juliet*, a drama Shakespeare was working on at the same time as *A Midsummer Night's Dream*. Use the grid below to compare the fate of these ill-fated lovers.

Question:	Hermia & Lysander	Pyramus & Thisbe	Romeo & Juliet
Who is against their marriage and why?			
How do they attempt to overcome the opposition to their love?			
Does the plan work?			
What is the outcome?			
What is the main reason for this outcome?			

OBEDIENCE
"As she is mine, I may dispose of her"

In Shakespeare's time, society was much stricter, revolving around a number of bonds of kinship as well as obedience. Depending upon who they were and where they lived, different people had different duties and responsibilities. While the feudal system had come to an end, lords would still have a huge staff of servants who were required to be obedient and loyal.

In society, the position of women was not strong, and they were expected to look after the household (staff) and support their husbands. In all things they were expected to obey their husbands, who had total control over them. While there are examples of independent women (Queen Elizabeth I being the most remarkable one), this was the exception and not the rule. The male dominance is obvious in the play: Egeus can dispose of his daughter as he sees fit, even put her to death – a right that Theseus upholds; Theseus is preparing to marry a warrior woman, turning her from a figure of female power into a calm and silent housewife, waiting upon his pleasure; in the final Act, after marriage, all the women (with the sometime exception of Hippolyta) have fallen strangely (and uncomfortably) silent.

At the time the play was written (1595), all people were expected to be loyal to the sovereign and to obey her. The sovereign was at the top of society and therefore claimed the highest of all the various duties and loyalties that bound society. Thus, in the world of the play, Theseus is the person who holds all bonds of obedience together: the Mechanicals perform for him (and wish to please him), the lovers are subject to his will and law, as is Egeus, who has to accept that his will concerning his daughter has been overruled.

Some ideas for activities:

- Pupils can be asked to draw a chart showing bonds of obedience. Characters in this would be grouped in a pyramid, showing allegiances and how they affect the characters in the play.

- In Act IV Scene 1, Bottom thoroughly enjoys his role as lover of the fairy queen, and he commands various fairies to carry out duties for him. Pupils could be asked to write a playscript containing some further instructions, detailing how the fairies wait on him and react to the mortal's strange wishes.

- Pupils can be asked to draw two pictures of Hippolyta: one before her defeat by Theseus, showing her as an independent warrior, the other after her marriage, emphasizing how she has been turned into an obedient queen. The clothing as well as her posture should show the change.

WHO MUST OBEY WHOM?
"Your servant shall do so"

Fill in the names of the following characters in the chart below and show how obedience and dominance are displayed in the play.

Hermia, Puck, Lysander, Demetrius, Titania, Hippolyta, Theseus, Oberon, Egeus

The Athenians

The Fairies

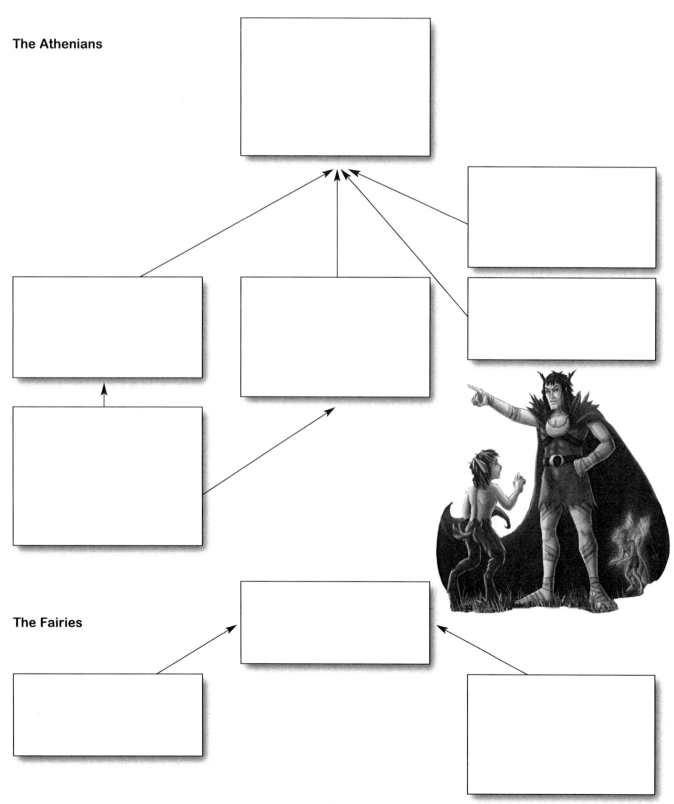

DREAMS AND IMAGINATION
"What visions have I seen!"

Dreams are another major preoccupation of *A Midsummer Night's Dream*. Indeed, with such a title, it would be strange if the play did not deal with dreams to a certain degree. Having said that, although the play contains numerous references to dreams and dreaming, there is only one real dream in it: Hermia's in Act II Scene 2 of having a serpent eating her heart.

Dreams, it seems, were something that preoccupied Shakespeare throughout his life, particularly at the time of writing *A Midsummer Night's Dream*. *Romeo and Juliet*, in the famous Queen Mab speech of Mercutio, contains a detailed description of the "fairies' midwife" that brings humans their dreams. Here the themes of fairies and dreams combine.

Although there is only one dream in *A Midsummer Night's Dream*, a number of characters at various times in the play profess to having dreamt, or of their experience resembling a dream. Thus, wide stretches of the play can be seen as having a dreamlike quality – at least for the characters involved. But we, as audience, also share in this dreamlike quality, as we are instructed by Puck to suppose the whole play was "but a dream" if we didn't like it.

Linked to the idea of dreams, understood as "wishful thinking," is the notion of the imagination – what we see with our mind's eye. *A Midsummer Night's Dream* is the play in which Shakespeare most often uses the word "eye" – surely no coincidence. Cupid is blind, and the love juice is smeared on the eyes. With their direct connection to the brain, the eyes to a large degree control what we think and desire.

Some ideas for activities:

- The word "dream" keeps cropping up at important stages of the play. The pupils could be asked to analyze what the dream imagery in each case suggests.

- Similarly, the ideas of "eyes" and looking with someone else's eyes recur again and again. Students can be asked to analyze who sees with whose eyes at certain stages, and how the vision is "restored" (if at all).

- In the epilogue, the audience is asked to think the whole play was "but a dream" if they didn't like it. To what extent could the play be seen as a dream? What elements of a dream appear in the play? And is a dream something positive or negative? (the epilogue seems to suggest a dream is not to be taken seriously). The pupils could also examine what positive and negative aspects a dream might have, and how those tie in with the play.

- Hermia's dream seems to warn her of Lysander's leaving her. What dream might Egeus have on the night of Hermia fleeing the house? Pupils who are particularly gifted could try writing the dream in iambic pentameter.

I SPY WITH MY LITTLE EYE
"Your eyes must with his judgment look"

In the play, a number of characters are either asked to see things differently (i.e. through the eyes of another) or they have a view that conflicts with another's. Use the chart below to note whose eyes each character looks with (or is asked to see the world with) and what the effect of this is, or should be.

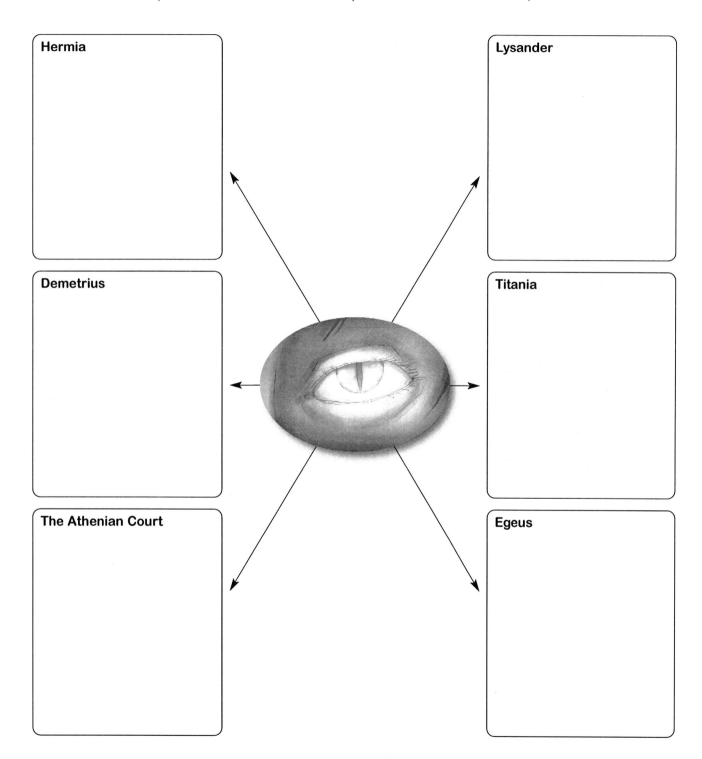

Hermia

Lysander

Demetrius

Titania

The Athenian Court

Egeus

WHO IS DREAMING WHAT?

"Four nights will quickly dream away the time"

In *A Midsummer Night's Dream*, a number of characters refer to dreams they thought they had or actually did have – which underlines the dreamlike quality of the whole play. Why all these references to dreams? Use the grid below to help you explore the various dreams.

Who does the dream apply to?	Evidence from the text & content of the dream	Relevance of the dream
Theseus (I.1)		
Hermia (II.2)		
Lovers (IV.1)		

WHO IS DREAMING WHAT?

(cont'd)

Who does the dream apply to?	Evidence from the text & content of the dream	Relevance of the dream
Bottom (IV.1)		
Titania (IV.1)		
Audience (epilogue)		

THE MOON – MADNESS AND CHASTITY
"The moon, methinks, looks with a wat'ry eye"

As one would expect of a play with "dream" in the title, a lot of the action takes place at night. This might explain why there are frequent references to the moon. However, the moon is not only mentioned when the characters talk about meeting in the woods – a large number of the references to the moon pertain to the Mechanicals staging *Pyramus and Thisbe* and the difficulties they have of credibly showing moonshine on stage. The remaining references deal with the more troubling aspects of the moon and its goddess, Diana. In a play that revolves mainly around love and marriage, Shakespeare uses moon imagery to show the opposite side: celibacy and chastity.

As Shakespeare wrote the play during the reign of Elizabeth I, widely known as the Virgin Queen, he could not paint too negative a picture of chastity. Indeed, while chastity is presented as undesirable to the male dominated court and the young Hermia, Titania (though not chaste) is linked more closely to the ideas and ideals of chastity, both through the episode of her votaress and the fact that Oberon restores her sight to a more chaste view of the world (although, unlike suggested of Elizabeth I, she is not immune to the power of the love-in-idleness, nor to Cupid's arrow).

Another aspect of the moon that is briefly explored is its affinity to lunacy. This name for madness stems from the belief that the moon and its varying phases could influence people's behavior. Indeed, the play somehow suggests that the chaotic goings-on of the night are more akin to madness than anything else. The characters involved all believe they have been dreaming, but Theseus insists it must be some form of madness; we, the audience, know it is the folly of being in love.

Some ideas for activities:

- Pupils can be asked to explore the references to the moon that are more than mere references to night-time or the Mechanicals' staging difficulties. The idea here should be to find out what each quotation signifies and how it fits in with the themes of the play.

- Theseus's speech on poets, madmen and lovers (in V.1) is central to the idea of lunacy and is worth exploring in detail. Particular emphasis should be placed on how Theseus means to disparage all three but somehow gives them a positive spin, especially when referring to poets.

CHASTE DIANA
"Chanting faint hymns to the cold fruitless moon"

Use the following grid to explore some of Shakespeare's moon-related imagery.

Extract	What does the extract mean?
Theseus, bewailing the fact that time passes too slowly until his wedding day (I.1) but, O, methinks, how slow This old moon wanes! She lingers my desires, Like to a step-dame, or a dowager, Long withering out a young man's revenue.	
Theseus, describing to Hermia what fate awaits her, should she disobey her father (I.1) For aye to be in shady cloister mew'd, To live a barren sister all your life, Chanting faint hymns to the cold fruitless moon.	
Oberon, describing how the flower "love-in-idleness" gained its power from Cupid's arrow (II.1) And loos'd his love-shaft smartly from his bow, As it should pierce a hundred thousand hearts. But I might see young Cupid's fiery shaft Quench'd in the chaste beams of the wat'ry moon	
Titania, enamored, before she retires with Bottom (III.1) The moon, methinks, looks with a watery eye; And when she weeps, weeps every little flower, Lamenting some enforced chastity.	
Oberon, applying the cure for the love potion into Titania's eyes (IV.1) Be, as thou wast wont to be; See, as thou wast wont to see: Dian's bud o'er Cupid's flower Hath such force and blessed power.	

THESEUS'S SPEECH ON LOVERS, POETS AND MADMEN
"But man is but a patched fool"

Theseus, commenting on the strange story of the lovers, delivers an important speech about lovers, madmen, poets and the imagination. Use this sheet to explore what Theseus is saying, and how his criticism somehow sounds positive.

> Note the many references to eyes and seeing – how does this relate to the rest of the play?

> Why would a madman see devils? What connotation does this give to the madman?

> Does "cool reason" sound positive or negative? Explain.

Lovers and madmen have such seething brains,

Such shaping fantasies, that apprehend

More than cool reason ever comprehends.

The lunatic, the lover, and the poet,

Are of imagination all compact:

One sees more devils than vast hell can hold;

That is the madman: the lover, all as frantic,

Sees Helen's beauty in a brow of Egypt:

The poet's eye, in a fine frenzy rolling,

Doth glance from heaven to earth, from earth to heaven;

And, as imagination bodies forth

The forms of things unknown, the poet's pen

Turns them to shapes, and gives to airy nothing

A local habitation, and a name.

Such tricks hath strong imagination,

That, if it would but apprehend some joy,

It comprehends some bringer of that joy:

Or, in the night, imagining some fear,

How easy is a bush suppos'd a bear?

> Who is the Helen being referred to here? The one from the play, or another? Why Egypt?

> What does the poet do with his pen?

> Is the poet more like the lover or the madman?

> Do these last lines refer to poets only, or to all three? Explain.

> What do the words "frantic" and "frenzy" suggest?

ANALYTICAL ESSAYS

Writing an analytical essay on a theme involves looking at the whole play and discovering how the theme develops, including any build-up and resolution.

To write an analytical essay successfully, it is suggested that pupils use the P-E-E-L structure.
PEEL stands for:

P-oint   Stating the argument.

E-vidence   The evidence for the point, using quotations where applicable.

E-xplain   A deeper explanation of the argument, taking the evidence into account, relative to the
                    theme and the essay title.

L-ink   Reinforce the Point at the end, linking all arguments back to the beginning.

To prepare an essay using this technique, isolate key scenes that deal with the theme and explore each scene with reference to the essay title. These scenes, using quotations where appropriate, will form the backbone of your essay, as they provide the evidence for the arguments.

In order to avoid rambling, it is important that the analysis of the scenes is geared solely toward the title. Similarly, no more than three scenes should be explored in any depth.

The scenes selected do not have to prove the same point – indeed, it is often better to present different views, all of which support (or contradict) the argument, bringing the points together in the conclusion of the essay.

The following worksheets are presented to aid in the preparation of analytical essays:

*   Charting the development of a theme throughout the play;

*   Exploring a theme by briefly analyzing a number of key scenes generally (not bound to an essay title);

*   Planning sheet for an analytical essay, including the deeper analysis of three scenes.

Image from Classical Comics' The Tempest.
Artwork by: Jon Haward and Gary Erskine

71

THEME EXPLORATION SHEET

Use the following worksheet to help order your thoughts on the theme of your choice.

THEME:

Select a scene in which the theme is central

Summarize the scene briefly, using quotations where appropriate, focusing on how the theme is present.	What does the scene tell us about the theme? Note down all observations that are connected to the theme.

If possible, select another scene in which the theme is central or present.

Summarize the scene briefly, using quotations where appropriate, focusing on how the theme is present.	What does the scene tell us about the theme? Note down all observations that are connected to the theme.

If possible, select a third scene in which the theme is central or present.

Summarize the scene briefly, using quotations where appropriate, focusing on how the theme is present.	What does the scene tell us about the theme? Note down all observations that are connected to the theme.

If possible, select a fourth scene in which the theme is central or present.

Summarize the scene briefly, using quotations where appropriate, focusing on how the theme is present.	What does the scene tell us about the theme? Note down all observations that are connected to the theme.

ESSAY WRITING FRAME

Use the framework to help you organize your ideas for an essay on the theme of your choice.

TITLE OF ESSAY (the statement)

First paragraph: **Introduction**
Briefly discuss the statement. What are the main points? Link the statement to the play.

Second paragraph: Illustrate the statement with an example.	
Find a passage in the play that can be used as an example for the point you're trying to make.	What does this passage show in relation to the statement?

Third paragraph: illustrate the statement with a second example.	
Find a scene in the play that can be used as an example for the point you're trying to make.	What does this passage show in relation to the statement?

Fourth paragraph: Use a third example to illustrate the statement.	
Find a part in the play that can be used as an example for the point you're trying to make.	What does this passage show in relation to the statement?

Fifth paragraph: **Conclusion** – your opinion.	
Does the statement hold true or not? Perhaps it is only occasionally true?	Briefly re-cap the main points and finish with your own opinion.

POSSIBLE ESSAY TITLES

Based on the main themes in *A Midsummer Night's Dream*, the following is a selection of possible essay titles centered around each theme.

Love and Marriage

1. In what way is the love between Theseus and Hippolyta, Titania and Oberon and the lovers different?
2. To what extent does reason govern the choice of marriage partner in *A Midsummer Night's Dream*? Focus also on Egeus's choice of husband for Hermia.
3. Lysander says, "The course of true love never did run smooth." To what extent is this exemplified in *A Midsummer Night's Dream*?
4. If not for the love potion, *A Midsummer Night's Dream* would not have a happy ending. Discuss this statement, making reference to either the *Pyramus and Thisbe* story or *Romeo and Juliet*.
5. Based on the evidence of *A Midsummer Night's Dream*, what is Shakespeare's idea of the role of women in marriage?
6. The "roundel" of the lovers in the woods shows how fickle love can be. Do you think that the lovers can be happy after all that has happened to them in the woods?

Obedience

1. Why does Titania cease her strife with Oberon after he has removed the enchantment from her?
2. What lessons about obedience and duty can we learn from Egeus? Think not only about his obedience to Theseus, but also about Hermia.
3. Puck and Oberon are servant and master. What kind of a relationship is it exactly? What does it tell us about obedience and servitude generally?
4. Both Theseus and Oberon rule their respective kingdoms strictly, expecting absolute obedience. Discuss.

Dreams

1. What does *A Midsummer Night's Dream* with its multiple (supposed) dreams suggest about the nature of dreams?
2. In what way is Hermia's dream of the snake prophetic, and why is she the only person to have a warning dream?
3. In what way might it be helpful, as an audience, to imagine that the whole play was just a dream?
4. In what way does the fact that they think the happenings in the wood were just a dream affect the lovers and also Theseus and Hippolyta?

Imagination

1. Do you agree that sight is the most important sense in love? Use evidence from *A Midsummer Night's Dream* in your answer.
2. In what way is the Mechanicals' use of props and roles in their play ironic? You might wish to focus on their thoughts regarding killing and lions on stage as well as the wall and the moon.
3. To what extent might the audience believe that the whole fairy realm is nothing but a figment of the imagination? And if so, whose imagination?
4. To what extent do you think that Puck can be seen as an embodiment of the imagination?

The Moon (Madness and Chastity)

1. In what ways does *A Midsummer Night's Dream* suggest that marriage is preferable to chastity?
2. To what extent can the female characters in the play be regarded as embodiments of chastity?
3. The moon is generally seen as a symbol of women. To what extent does *A Midsummer Night's Dream* reflect this idea?
4. Love is a form of madness. Discuss.
5. Although the mad goings-on in the wood are due to the juice of the flower, it is equally possible that they could have happened without any magical intervention. Argue for and against this proposition.
6. In what way can writing poetry or plays be seen as "a fine frenzy"? In your answer, you should also discuss the connotations of the phrase, relating your arguments to *A Midsummer Night's Dream*.

DRAMA ACTIVITIES

Introduction

Because *A Midsummer Night's Dream* is a play, any intense involvement with the text – to be successful – must involve acting of some sort. Pupils don't need to act out the whole play or even entire scenes to get a flavor of the piece. Short, focused drama exercises can help engage with the play as it was intended.

There are a number of general drama techniques that can be used in various circumstances and adapted to suit the focus of the lesson. The most important of these are:

Freeze Framing

A group of pupils are asked to recreate a scene. They are given some time to work out where to position the characters, what expression their faces should show, and what gestures to make. Then, when the teacher says "freeze," they must get into the correct positions and hold the freeze, basically forming a three-dimensional photo (rather like a panel in the graphic novel).

Pupils can be unfrozen a group at a time to give them a chance to look at what other pupils have done. This allows a brief discussion / peer review about what makes a particular freeze effective.

You may wish to extend this technique by allowing frozen characters to briefly describe what they are thinking.

Hot-Seating

This is a drama technique particularly suited to exploring character and motivation. One pupil is chosen to play the part of a character from the text (e.g. Demetrius), and the rest of the class asks questions, which the pupil has to answer as he/she believes that character would.

The questions should be fired quite quickly, much like at a news conference, challenging the hot-seated pupil's thinking as well as their ability to build up a credible character around the information contained in the play.

Repetition of Phrases

A very good way of gauging the effectiveness of language and the pitch of a delivery is to take a short phrase and repeat it in as many different ways as possible, e.g. angrily, joyfully, spitefully, worriedly, doubtfully. This will help the pupils to listen to their voices and modulate them according to mood, as well as discover which mood suits a certain line best. Recording this in audio only, or even video with audio, provides valuable feedback to the pupil.

Short Interchanges

Similar to extended freeze-frames, this is a great method for some very basic character acting. Pupils are paired up, and each is assigned a character and a small number of lines for an interaction. From those lines, each pupil selects one line that they feel best represents the main message from that character. The pupils then say their lines in turn, trying to put as much emphasis as possible into their selected lines, using gestures and facial expressions. In that way, they distill their given character into one line and a gesture. Developments of relationship can also be explored using this technique, by choosing lines that follow the play's development.

Short Speech

Asking pupils to prepare a short speech (e.g. Egeus's or Hippolyta's) is an ideal way of developing speaking skills. Ideally, pupils would memorize the extract so that they can give a good delivery (without a sheet obstructing their connection with the audience). This would also enable them to add more gestures and facial expression to their delivery, deepening their character acting. It is a great idea to record the pupils as

DRAMA ACTIVITIES

(cont'd)

they speak, using video equipment. Playing this back to them and discussing what they did well and what they need to work on, based on the impartial evidence of a recording, is one of the best ways to improve speaking skills.

More advanced techniques include:

Mime

Pupils often struggle with how to act without talking; how to behave when on stage but not actually delivering any lines. Exercises that involve mime are a great way to help overcome this difficulty. It is possible to mime simple emotions and even act out a whole scene without saying a word. Alternatively, a teacher or a pupil could read the lines, with the other pupils acting along without saying a word.

Improvisation

This technique requires courage and a detailed knowledge of the characters. It is therefore best combined with character work. The technique involves putting the characters into a scene and asking them to act the scene out straight away, with no preparation. Harrowing as this experience can be for some pupils, it encourages quick thinking, staying in role, and character study.

Some ideas for activities involving drama techniques include:

- Hot-seat Egeus after I.1. Questions should revolve around why he is so eager for his daughter to marry Demetrius, what he has against Lysander, and why he would be willing to have his daughter killed if she disobeys him.

- Hot-seat Oberon after his resolve to make Titania pay for her disobedience in II.1. Questions should revolve around why he wants the Indian boy so much, why he does not accept Titania's explanation, why he wishes to punish her so cruelly, and why he thinks he is in the right.

- Hot-seat the lovers after they have woken from their experience in the woods (IV.1). They should be questioned on what they remember, how they view the events, and how they can explain them.

- Select a number of opposing characters (Helena – Demetrius, Titania – Oberon) or characters in dialogue (Oberon – Puck, Bottom – Quince) and give each character only one line to say. Split the class into two groups and assign each group one of the roles. Each pupil is to say their line emphatically, with one gesture.

- Egeus does not have a lot to say. In particular at the end, he is overruled and is not allowed to plead his case. This makes the scene a good test-piece to explore mime and other forms of non-verbal reaction to what is being said.

- Freeze-frame the ten most important scenes. Pupils can either make up their own list of ten, or the list could be drawn up together in class (which also allows for a comparison of freezes). After the pupils are given sufficient time to prepare, freeze all ten moments in succession. Keep the best freeze each time for other pupils to see and (when unfrozen) to comment on the freeze's effectiveness.

It is often useful to group pupils for drama activities and to have one pupil as "director" or coach, helping the other pupils to achieve their shared vision.

CHARACTERISTIC ONE-LINERS
"There is not one word apt"

TASK:

Below is a selection of one-liners from various characters. First match up the lines to the characters, and then try to capture that person's characteristics in how she or he says the line.

Characters	One-liners
Theseus	The fairy land buys not the child of me
Hippolyta	If I do it, let the audience look to their eyes
Egeus	I love thee not, therefore pursue me not
Oberon	Nay, faith, let me not play a woman; I have a beard coming
Titania	Have you the lion's part written? pray you, if it be, give it me, for I am slow of study
Puck	You can never bring in a wall
Bottom	I am, my lord, as well deriv'd as he
Quince	But, O, methinks, how slow this old moon wanes
Flute	I know not by what power I am made bold
Starveling	I will fawn on you: use me but as your spaniel
Snout	I never heard so musical a discord, such sweet thunder
Snug	I am that merry wanderer of the night
Helena	All that I have to say, is, to tell you that the lantern is the moon; I, the man i' the moon
Hermia	Thou shalt not from this grove, till I torment thee for this injury
Lysander	But, masters, here are your parts
Demetrius	I beg the ancient privilege of Athens

DEVELOPING RELATIONSHIPS
"Some true love turn'd, and not a false turn'd true"

One-liners can also be used to chart how a relationship between two characters develops. The following one-liners trace the relationship between Oberon and Titania, and Demetrius and Helena. Apart from acting them out and seeing how the relationship changes, you can also analyze who says what, and who usually starts the dialogue, discerning what this might tell you about the characters and their relationship.

Oberon: Ill met by moonlight, proud Titania	**Titania:** What, jealous Oberon! Fairies, skip hence
Titania: And this same progeny of evils comes From our debate, from our dissension	**Oberon:** Why should Titania cross her Oberon?
Oberon: I do but beg a little changeling boy	**Titania:** The fairy land buys not the child of me
Oberon (to himself): thou shalt not from this grove, Till I torment thee for this injury	(no response from Titania)
Oberon: What thou seest, when thou dost wake, Do it for thy true-love take	**Titania (to herself, about Bottom):** What angel wakes me from my flowery bed?
Oberon (spoken to Puck): And now I have the boy, I will undo This hateful imperfection of her eyes	**Titania:** My Oberon! what visions have I seen! Methought, I was enamour'd of an ass
Oberon: Sound, music! Come, my queen, take hands with me	**Titania:** Come, my lord; and in our flight, Tell me how it came this night
Titania: Hand in hand, with fairy grace, Will we sing, and bless this place	**Oberon:** Now, until the break of day, Through this house each fairy stray

Helena (spoken to Hermia): O, teach me how you look, and with what art You sway the motion of Demetrius' heart	(no response from Demetrius)
Demetrius: I love thee not, therefore pursue me not	**Helena:** Use me but as your spaniel, spurn me, strike me
Demetrius: I'll run from thee, and hide me in the brakes	**Helena:** We cannot fight for love, as men may do; We should be woo'd, and were not made to woo
Demetrius: O Helen, goddess, nymph, perfect, divine!	**Helena:** O spite; O hell! I see you all are bent To set against me for your merriment
Helena: I pray you, though you mock me, gentlemen, Let her not hurt me	**Demetrius:** She shall not
Demetrius: The object and the pleasure of mine eye, Is only Helena	**Helena:** I have found Demetrius, like a jewel, Mine own, and not mine own

ACTING OUT SCENES FROM THE PLAY
"Say, what abridgement have you for this evening?"

Acting out scenes in class is always a challenge – in a variety of ways. Discipline can be an issue (especially as excitement mounts), so it is important to establish clear rules and procedures for when pupils need to pay attention. The greatest problems will probably be the amount of space and keeping all pupils involved. Three scenes (or part-scenes) in *A Midsummer Night's Dream* are particularly suited to being acted out in class. These are the meeting of Titania and Oberon (II.1), Titania doting on Bottom (IV.1), and the performance of the Mechanicals' play (V.1). All these scenes can be staged in a way that involves all pupils (if necessary in two parallel groups), and they each present different challenges. Act II Scene 1 has two very strong characters clashing, while their respective fairy trains have nothing to say but must contribute in some way to the atmosphere of conflict and unclear loyalty; Act IV Scene 1 has a host of fairies either attending to Bottom's wishes or commenting on the situation through miming; Act V Scene 1 has the Mechanicals presenting their play with the court of Athens looking on – while the Mechanicals speak, the whole court must react to what they see.

Act II Scene 1:

Two things should be borne in mind here. Firstly, while only Titania and Oberon speak, they enter with their servant fairies, who need to do something while the two main characters fight it out. Secondly, Titania talks of nature being in discord, and this could be represented in some way to underline her case. The atmosphere that should be brought across is one of turmoil and upheaval.

Some ideas on how to stage the scene:

- The fairies in each train could support their ruler and act as though they would pick a fight with any fairy of the other ruler's train – much like gangs sizing each other up. Alternatively, they could act surprised and at a loss of how to deal with this sudden and heated argument between their rulers.
- Some pupils could be dressed as trees or flowers, and their contortions could mirror the turmoil in nature.
- Make use of the music department to find percussion instruments that can simulate a storm (drums, cymbals etc.). Lighting will be more difficult, but darkening the room and using flashlights with a strobe function would be effective.
- There should be real venom between the two actors playing Oberon and Titania – lovers' spats are usually ugly, and this one is no exception. Remember Titania is not a lightweight, but a commanding queen who actually gets the better of Oberon in this encounter.

ACTING OUT SCENES FROM THE PLAY

(cont'd)

Act IV Scene 1:

In this scene, Bottom, who does not know he has a donkey's head on his neck, feels more at home as the fairy queen's lover and orders the fairies around. They obey him, of course, but one wonders whether they do this freely or grudgingly. Once again, we have two main characters and a host of fairies in attendance with silent parts.

Some ideas on how to stage the scene:

- Bottom calls for music. What kind of music might the fairies play him? Here you could use the resources of the music department to create fairy sounds.

- Titania is obviously in love with Bottom. How does she express this? We know she strokes him, but how else might she show her total adulation for the "translated" Bottom?

- How does Bottom act in all this? He sends four fairies on various missions – how does he ask them to do this? Is he full of his power and exercising it just to show he can? Or is he only asking the fairies for help?

- How do the fairies being asked to do chores react? Are they eager to please their queen and thereby also Bottom? Or do they resent having to work for a donkey-headed mortal and show this, as far as they dare?

- What do the other fairies make of their mistress's new love? How do they show what they think of this liaison?

Act V Scene 1:

Here the entire Athenian court, which has celebrated the triple wedding, watches the play staged by the Mechanicals. This is a key comic scene; if it is to be effective, not only must the Mechanicals act well and their timing be impeccable, but all other onlookers must add to the atmosphere of hilarity.

Some ideas on how to stage the scene:

- For this scene you have to think about where the Mechanicals act and how the court will watch them, at the same time ensuring that the real audience can see both groups.

- Only the Athenian men (Theseus, Lysander and Demetrius) and Hippolyta comment on the play. All other onlookers (in particular Hermia and Helena) do not speak. Does this mean they have to be silent? How could they show their reaction to the Mechanicals?

- How do the Mechanicals react to the mockery of the court, which they can hear? Does it make them say their lines more quickly, to get it over and done with, or more emphatically, in a bid to win the audience over? Or are they so lost in their own performance that they do not react to it?

- What do the Mechanicals that are not "on stage" do? Do they immerse themselves in the performance of their colleagues? Or do they groan and realize how bad their play is?

- Both Pyramus's and Thisbe's final speeches are full of linguistic humor. Does this transfer onto the actors? Or does one of the Mechanicals manage to evoke real feelings for his character?

These are suggestions on these three scenes, but any scene can be adapted for acting out in the classroom. The more time and effort you put into a "mini-production," the more rewarding it will be; and the more pupils will gain from the experience of exploring play scripts for themselves and bringing their own personal slants to a text.

WORD JUMBLE

Solve the following anagrams to find the names of characters or things to do with *A Midsummer Night's Dream*.

Jumbled Spelling	Correct Spelling
Slay nerd	
Tiered Sum	
She Suet	
Happy Toil	
He I Mar	
An Heel	
She Tan	
Hotplate Sir	
Ron Beo	
I At A Nit	
Wool Go Fled	
To Tomb	
Nic Que	
Grist V Lane	
Guns	
Not Us	
Clang Hinge	
Seated Drums	
Lame Boss Pose	
Ebb Cow	
DI Puc	
Ms Mire Mud	
Things	
Armed	
She Peaks Ear	

CROSSWORD

ACROSS

4   Theseus is Duke of this (6)
6   The leader of the acting group:
     Peter _____ (6)
10 The fairy king (6)
11 The _____ boy, whom the Fairy King and
     Queen argue about (10)
16 An Act I Scene 1, how many days until the
     wedding? (4)
18 Snug's role in the Mechanicals' play (4)
20 The name of the magical flower (4,2,8)
22 The play performed for the Duke: *Pyramus and*
     _____ (6)
23 The name of the song that Bottom will ask to be
     written: Bottom's _____ (5)
24 Hermia's father (5)

DOWN

1   The "god" whose arrow hit the flower (5)
2   Hermia's friend and occasional love-rival (6)
3   Puck's real name (5,10)
5   The fairy queen (7)
7   The boy whom Hermia's father wants her to
     marry (9)
8   The type of head put on Bottom by Puck (6)
9   The weather element created by Puck so that the
     lovers become lost in the forest (3)
12 Theseus's fiancée, who was Queen of the
     Amazons
13 The part played by Snout, separating the lovers
     in the Mechanicals' play (4)
14 Duke Theseus hunts with these (6)
15 Hermia's true love (8)
17 Theseus opts not to hear this at the end of the
     Mechanicals' play (8)
19 What Hermia dreams eats away her heart (5)
21 "The course of true love never did
     run_____" (6)
23 Canine companion to the man in the moon (3)

WORD SEARCH

The following words are hidden in the grid below. Words can be horizontal, vertical, or diagonal, and they may run in any direction (forward or backward).

ATHENS	SNOUT	MUSTARDSEED	HELENA
HOBGOBLIN	COBWEB	THESEUS	PHILOSTRATE
QUINCE	MOONSHINE	FAIRY	WALL
BOTTOM	SNUG	OBERON	HERMIA
HOUNDS	DEMETRIUS	THISBE	PUCK
ROBINGOODFELLOW	MOTE	FLUTE	HIPPOLYIA
CHANGELING	STARVELING	PEASEBLOSSOM	PYRAMUS
LYSANDER	EGEUS	TITANIA	

```
Z U I K Z B C M A O J O S A T H E N S Q W P
G P T P G E V K C U P A I M R E H S X E N X
W H Y I B E N F T B J H H P I Q L O K D F S
Y I G H N S F S G F L D Q T E B X G P J N E
W L S C O B W E B V E B R N R P E I T O L T
L O U R Z O V U N E A X M O A J I S U S J C
L S E X L N M I S C R T B O F E P T T A V N
W T G N J J L D H Z D I Y X T S V A O V T W
B R E P Y B R A L U N S D L A E R E S A Q A
N A Y L O A N E H G F I D I O V A N F G J P
E T F G T G N S O K V T N M E P U B P F E Y
Y E B S E M U O L E H A H L O G P E F S N R
M O U L T M D Y T E T I I I X O A I N N O I
H M I E A F Y U S I B N Q R S S N O H H R A
P N F R E C L E T X G E Z Q E B N S L I E F
G F Y L H F U N M W V O H B I D E X H M B E
N P L C F S C H G M F E L R P A N C P I O F
I O X V Z A M E O Z L O C S B G U A W L N J
W H O U N D S T S E S C C X Y U L F S A F E
A A O E E Z T T N S G V K Z R E R I D Y L R
W O C A T O M A O D E M E T R I U S I Q L L
F R X A B H L M Q U I N C E W Q W J S U M O
```

83

THE ENDING OF *A MIDSUMMER NIGHT'S DREAM*
TEACHERS' VERSION

Solution (page 10)

Question	A Midsummer Night's Dream	The Tempest	All's Well That Ends Well	As You Like It
Who delivers the Prologue?	**Puck, a minor character of mischief**	**Prospero, the main character**	**King, a minor character**	**Rosalind, a female, the main character**
Is the actor in character?	**Yes, but aware that he is talking to an audience.**	**Debatable – at the beginning he seems to be in character; when addressing audience mixture of Prospero and actor.**	**no, he speaks as an actor who is no longer the king but a "beggar".**	**no, philosophizes about the structure of plays and the worth of epilogues.**
How is the character trying to persuade the audience to clap?	**No persuasion, more argument: if the audience is dissatisfied, it was all a dream, if they are satisfied, they should clap.**	**Imploring them to release him from island through the clapping as he has no more magic. Wind produced by hands will propel his sails.**	**Title of the play is not true until audience claps; actors at mercy of audience.**	**Appealing to men and women to persuade each other; the promise of a kiss from her.**
How does the epilogue relate to the rest of the play?	**Puck says that if audience didn't like the play they should imagine it was a dream – epilogue thus keys in to the main theme and calls the whole experience of the play into question.**	**Prospero, who has controlled the whole plot of the play, is now powerless as he has renounced his magic. As he has become a normal man, so the play must end and he must rely on the audience to "save" him.**	**Not really – this is a stock epilogue. It only relates to title of the play that the play can't really end well (although it has) unless the audience approve of it.**	**Throughout the play Rosalind has been gently steering the play to its happy resolution. It is therefore fitting that she is also the one to solicit approval. Additionally, she plays upon all people being happily married in the play by appealing to women's and men's love.**

COMPREHENSION TESTS
TEACHERS' VERSION

Solution (pages 14-16)

Act I

Theseus, the **Duke** of Athens, can hardly wait to get married to **Hippolyta**, the Queen of the **Amazons**, whom he conquered in **battle**. Egeus disrupts their preparations and complains that his daughter, **Hermia**, will not obey his instructions and marry **Demetrius** because she loves **Lysander** instead. Theseus tells Hermia that, on the day of the royal wedding, she must decide either to marry as her father wishes, be executed, or become a **nun** forever. Lysander and Hermia bewail their bad fortune and decide to **flee** from **Athens**. They tell Hermia's friend Helena all about their intentions. **Helen** was once loved by Demetrius, before he loved Hermia. She still loves Demetrius and secretly decides to tell him of the lovers' **plan** to leave the town, in the hope of receiving some **thanks**.

Meanwhile, a group of simple **workmen** from Athens are planning to perform a **play** for the Duke's **wedding** celebrations. They plan on staging *Pyramus and* **Thisbe**, with Bottom as **Pyramus** and **Flute** as Thisbe, although **Bottom** wants to play all the parts in the play. They decide to meet in the **woods** the next night to rehearse.

Act II

Robin Goodfellow, otherwise known as **Puck**, meets a **fairy** in the woods. Both Titania and Oberon, the Queen and the King of the fairies, plan to be in the **woods** that night. However, the two are in conflict because **Titania** has an Indian child that **Oberon** wants, and she **refuses** to give it up. As a result of their **quarrel**, nature is in **turmoil**. Oberon is prepared to end the fight if Titania gives him the child. Her refusal makes Oberon vow to make her pay for her **disobedience**. He orders Puck to search out a **flower**, the juice of which makes people fall in love with the next thing they **see** when they wake, after it has been applied to the **eyes**. Oberon wants to make sure that Titania wakes up when something **vile** is near.

While Puck is gone, Oberon watches Demetrius and **Helena** walk through the woods in search of **Lysander** and Hermia. Demetrius continues to push Helena away. When Puck comes back to Oberon with the flower, in an attempt to set things right between Demetrius and Helena, he tells Puck to **anoint** the Athenian's eyes with the flower juice so that he will **love** the girl he **spurned**.

Elsewhere, Titania falls asleep, surrounded by her **fairy-court**. While asleep, Oberon smears some of the flower's **juice** onto her eyes.

In another part of the wood, Hermia and Lysander have lost their way; tired, they decide to sleep where they are. As they are not yet **married**, Hermia insists that they sleep **apart**. Puck, seeing them, thinks these are the two his master talked about, and he applies the juice onto **Lysander's** eyes. Helena stumbles into the area and wakes him. The magic of the flower has its effect, and he falls in love with her. Helena runs off, but Lysander **follows** her. After dreaming that a **snake** was eating her heart, Hermia wakes up alone.

Act III

Puck watches the **Mechanicals** rehearse their play and decides to have some fun with them. He puts a spell on **Bottom** so that his head becomes a **donkey**'s. When his friends see him, they run away. Left by himself, he **sings** to cheer himself up. The noise wakes **Titania**, who **falls in love** with him.

Puck reports all he has done to **Oberon**, who is **delighted**. **Demetrius** and Hermia enter, Hermia accusing him of having killed **Lysander**. Oberon realizes Puck has made a **mistake**. While Demetrius sleeps, exhausted from the night's events, Oberon puts the love juice on his eyes. **Helena** enters, followed by Lysander. Waking under the power of the potion, Demetrius sees Helena and falls in love with her; now both men **fight** over her. **Hermia** returns to the scene and accuses Helena of having **bewitched** Lysander. The two men go off to fight, and the two women leave separately.

Oberon is **angry** at Puck and tells him to set things right. Puck conjures up a dense **fog** in the wood and leads the two men **astray**. When they both fall asleep from **exhaustion**, Puck drips an **antidote** into **Lysander's** eyes. The two women, also tired from the night's happenings, arrive at the scene and, thinking they are alone, fall **asleep**, too.

COMPREHENSION TESTS
TEACHERS' VERSION

Solution (pages 17-18)

Act IV

Titania continues to be in love with the donkey-headed Bottom and asks her fairies to pander to his every **wish**. Oberon, who has meanwhile **taken** the Indian child from Titania, releases her from her **spell**. Titania wakes to see Bottom with the **donkey** head and realizes she has not been **dreaming**. The two make up and decide to **bless** Theseus's wedding.

Theseus and his court are out **hunting** in the morning, when they stumble upon the four lovers, who wake up to find that while **Lysander** loves **Hermia** again, **Demetrius** now loves **Helena**. **Egeus** still wants Hermia to marry Demetrius, but Theseus overrules him, seeing as the four are now **matched**. Theseus decides that the two **couples** will **marry** together with him and Hippolyta.

After they have left the scene, **Bottom** also wakes up, returned to his normal state and as **himself** again; but he cannot say what happened to him.

Back in Athens, the Mechanics are **distraught** without Bottom as they cannot **perform** the play without him. Suddenly he bursts in, and they are **overjoyed** and have **hope** again that their performance will go ahead.

Act V

Theseus and **Hippolyta** are not sure what to make of the lovers' **account** of the night's happenings. Philostrate, the master of the Duke's **revels** and entertainment, presents Theseus with a number of plays to **while** away the evening until bedtime. He chooses the Mechanicals' play of *Pyramus and Thisbe*.

All through the **performance**, the Athenians make fun of the **antics** and poor acting of the Mechanicals. Peter Quince, as prologue, gets his **punctuation** all wrong in his lines, saying the **opposite** of what he means. In the play, **Pyramus** (played by **Bottom**) and Thisbe (played by **Flute**) live next to each other and love one another, although their **parents** are against their love. They **communicate** through a chink or hole in the great wall that separates them, played by Snout. They agree to meet in secret outside the **city**. Thisbe arrives **first** at their meeting place and is **frightened** by a **lion** (played by Snug). She flees but leaves her scarf, which is **mauled** by the lion. When Pyramus arrives, he sees the mauled scarf and, believing that his beloved has been killed, **kills** himself. Thisbe **returns** and sees the **dead** Pyramus; distraught, she kills herself, too.

Theseus is **pleased** with the play and gives praise to the actors. After the play, they all go off to their **rooms**. When all have left, Oberon, Titania and their **fairies** fly through the house and **bless** its inhabitants.

Finally, at the end of the play, Puck enters, alone, and asks for **applause** or, if the audience did not enjoy the play, for them to imagine it was only a **dream**.

THE DIFFERENT WORLDS OF
A MIDSUMMER NIGHT'S DREAM
TEACHERS' VERSION

Solution (pages 19-20)

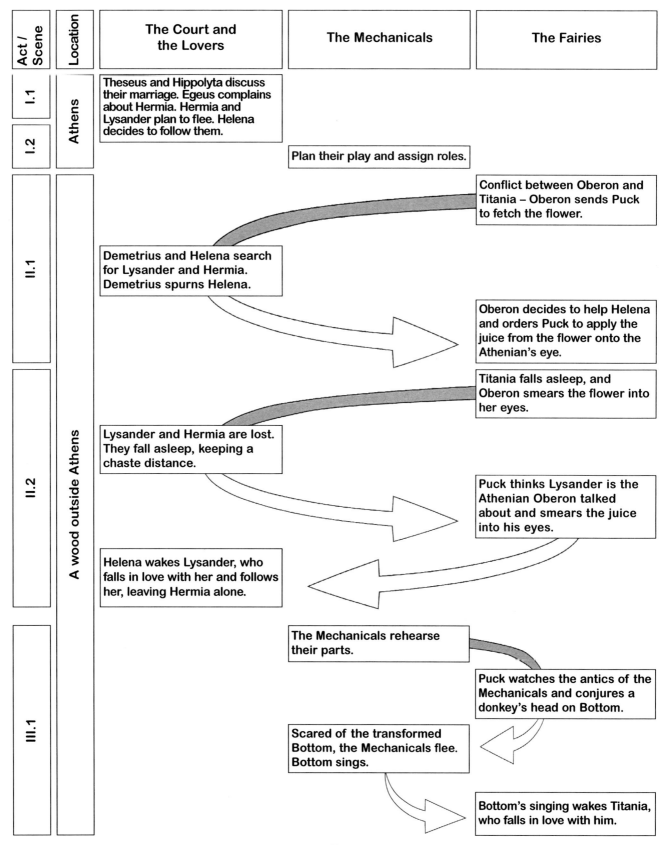

Act / Scene	Location	The Court and the Lovers	The Mechanicals	The Fairies
III.2	A wood outside Athens	Hermia believes Demetrius has killed Lysander. Demetrius lies down to sleep.		Oberon is pleased with Puck's work so far.
				Oberon realizes Puck's mistake and applies the juice into Demetrius's eyes. He orders Puck to bring Helena.
		Helena, followed by Lysander, enters. Demetrius falls in love with her. Helena thinks the men are making fun of her. Lysander tells Hermia he hates her; Hermia accuses Helena of bewitching Lysander. The men go off to fight.		
				Oberon orders Puck to set things right by applying the antidote to Lysander's eyes. Puck leads the men away from each other.
		Exhausted, all fall asleep.	Bottom is the beloved of Titania.	Titania continues to love Bottom, and they fall asleep together. Oberon puts the antidote into Titania's eyes, and she realizes what has happened. King and Queen make up and decide to bless the Duke's wedding.
IV.1		While out hunting, Theseus, Hippolyta and Egeus stumble upon the four lovers. Theseus overrules Egeus and decrees that all three couples will marry together.		
			Bottom wakes up and is at a loss to explain what happened.	
IV.2	Athens		The Mechanicals despair without Bottom. Bottom appears, and they prepare for the wedding.	
V.1	A wood outside Athens	Theseus and Hipolyta marvel at the lovers' story. Theseus chooses the Mechanicals' play. The Athenians interrupt the performance frequently to make witty asides. Theseus is pleased with the play, and all retire.	The Mechanicals perform *Pyramus and Thisbe.*	
Epilogue	A wood outside Athens			Oberon, Titania and the Fairies fly through the house and bless it. Puck closes the play by speaking directly to the audience.

SPOT THE DIFFERENCE
TEACHERS' VERSION

Solution (page 36)

HELENA		HERMIA
	short ——→	
	aggressive ——→	
←—— fair		
←—— lacking confidence		
←—— cautious, wary		
	assertive ——→	
	dark ——→	
←—— tall		
←—— loyal to her beloved ——→		
←—— lacking dignity		
←—— passive		
←—— selfless ——→		
betrays Hermia ◄- - - - - loyal ——→		
←—— rash ——→		
←—— trusting - - - -→ knows men to be fickle		

DEMETRIUS		LYSANDER
←—— affluent ——→		
←—— courageous ——→		
←—— inconstant		
←—— aristocratic ——→		
←—— eager to prove he's right ——→		
←—— assertive ——→		
←—— cruel		
←—— confident ——→		
←—— aggressive ——→		
	proactive ——→	
more mocking ←—— humorous, mocking ——→ more humorous		

DUKEDOM AND KINGDOM
TEACHERS' VERSION

Solution (page 37)

	The Athenian Court	The Fairy Court
What is the relationship between the rulers like?	Theseus has conquered Hippolyta and seems to love her, but we do not know whether she loves him. Theseus treats her with reverence and frequently asks her how she is. But he is the ruler and dominates her, if not quite as clearly as Oberon.	Oberon wants to dominate Titania. He is obviously passionate about Titania but needs to be very clear about who rules. The two are not on equal footing.
What problem(s) do they have?	1. Egeus complains that his daughter doesn't want to marry the man he has chosen for her. 2. Theseus needs to woo Hippolyta and convince her of his love Both problems revolve around accepting male authority.	Titania has a changeling boy whom Oberon wants. Because she refuses to give him up they argue, causing nature to be in turmoil. Once again, the problem is about accepting male authority.
How does Theseus / Oberon intend to solve the problem(s)	1. Gives Hermia 4 days to reach a decision. He does not want to go against Hermia's choice, but he must uphold the law, so he changes the penalty. 2. Plans on a grand wedding to impress Hippolyta.	1. Is sure to gain the boy from Titania and plans on punishing her for her disobedience. 2. Oberon also takes on solving Theseus's problem with the lovers, which he does with the help of the magical juice from the flower.
How are Theseus / Oberon's spirits lifted?	Theseus has no court jester that we know of. Philostrate is the master of his revels, and the Mechanicals keep him entertained after his wedding. But this entertainment is after the resolution of the conflict, not during, as with the Fairy Court.	Puck, Oberon's servant and jester, not only does Oberon's bidding, but in doing it also seeks to cheer him up. He achieves this with "creating" the monster that Titania falls in love with, although Oberon is not pleased with his confusion of the lovers.
How do they behave toward their subjects?	Theseus seems to care about his subjects – he does not want to comply with Egeus's wishes (ultimately overriding him), and he cares about the effort the Mechanicals put into their play.	Oberon is on good footing with Puck but knows that he needs to keep him on a short leash. His relationship with Titania's fairies (who are surely also his subjects) is less clear, but possibly hostile.
What might the Athenian Court learn from the Fairy Court?	Theseus appears tame and rational in comparison to Oberon. If Fairyland is a subconscious reflection of Athens, then Theseus is repressing his emotions. He needs to show more passion – also to win over Hippolyta. Theseus should possibly try to find more creative solutions to the problems he faces.	
What might the Fairy Court learn from the Athenian Court?	Oberon could learn to be more magnanimous and not dominate so aggressively (if he needs to dominate Titania). He should try to rule more fairly and consistently, rather than on a whim.	

THE RHYTHM OF SHAKESPEARE'S LANGUAGE
TEACHERS' VERSION

Solution (page 44)

X	>X<	X	>X<	X	>X<	X	>X<	X	>X<		
The	lun-	a-	tic,	the	lov-	er,	and	the	poet,		
Are	of	i-	mag-	in-	a-	tion	all	com-	pact:		
One	sees	more	de-	vils	than	vast	hell	can	hold;		
That	is	the	mad-	man:	the	lo-	ver,	all	as	fran-	tic,
Sees	He-	len's	beau-	ty	in	a	brow	of	E-	gypt:	
The	po-	et's	eye,	in	a	fine	fren-	zy	ro-	lling,	
Doth	glance	from	hea-	ven	to	earth,	from	earth	to	hea-	ven;
And	as	i-	mag-	in-	a-	tion	bo-	dies	forth		
The	forms	of	things	un-	known,	the	po-	et's	pen		
Turns	them	to	shapes	and	gives	to	air-	y	no-	thing	
A	lo-	cal	ha-	bi-	ta-	tion,	and	a	name		

QUINCE SPEAKS THE PROLOGUE
TEACHERS' VERSION

Solution (page 45)

If we offend, it is with our good will
that you should think we come, not to offend,
but with good will to show our simple skill:
that is the true beginning of our end.
Consider then, we come (but in despite
we do not come) as minding to content you.
Our true intent is all for your delight.
We are not here that you should here repent you.
The actors are at hand and by their show
you shall know all that you are like to know.

THE GROUPS AND THEIR LANGUAGE
TEACHERS' VERSION

Solution (pages 46-47)

The character's words	What does the poetic form tell us about the character?
ATHENIAN COURT	
THESEUS (talking to Hippolyta in Act I Scene 1) Now, fair Hippolyta, our nuptial hour Draws on apace: four happy days bring in Another moon; but, O, methinks, how slow This old moon wanes! she lingers my desires, Like to a step-dame, or a dowager, Long withering out a young man's revenue.	What can you say about the rhythm and rhyme? **blank verse: unrhymed iambic pentameter (5 stresses per line).** What effect does this mode of speaking have? **Slow rhythm without rhyme makes it sound serious and grave. Suits a ruler. Sounds like what he says is important, like he is someone who should be listened to.**
FAIRIES	
TITANIA (rebuking Oberon in Act II Scene 1) And never, since the middle summer's spring, Met we on hill, in dale, forest or mead, By paved fountain or by rushy brook, Or in the beached margent of the sea, To dance our ringlets to the whistling wind, But with thy brawls thou hast disturb'd our sport.	What can you say about the rhythm and rhyme? **almost pure iambic pentameter ("forest or mead" has an extra unstressed syllable in it), unrhymed; blank verse again (5 stresses per line).** What effect does this mode of speaking have? **As with Theseus, this form makes Titania sound serious. As she is arguing with Oberon, this form underlines the gravity of the argument and also her strong words and position.**
TITANIA (talking to her fairies in Act III Scene 1) Come, wait upon him; lead him to my bower. The moon, methinks, looks with a watery eye; And when she weeps, weeps every little flower, Lamenting some enforced chastity. Tie up my love's tongue, bring him silently.	What can you say about the rhythm and rhyme? **5 stresses per line again (iambic pentameter), but this time the lines rhyme: some are rhyming couplets.** What effect does this mode of speaking have? **This is more lyrical, more like a song. At home and with her lover, Titania sounds softer. She is in love, which might also explain the rhyme, which adds flow and softness.**
PUCK (alone in Act II Scene 2) Through the forest have I gone, But Athenian found I none, On whose eyes I might approve This flower's force in stirring love. Night and silence – who is here? Weeds of Athens he doth wear: This is he, my master said, Despised the Athenian maid; And here the maiden, sleeping sound, On the dank and dirty ground.	What can you say about the rhythm and rhyme? **4 stresses per line, basically iambic tetrameter, but many irregularities. Lines rhyme as rhyming couplets.** What effect does this mode of speaking have? **Four feet per line make the lines faster, more racy. This is underlined by the rhyming couplets, which speed the lines along. The whole atmosphere is of jerky (due to metrical irregularities) speed and quirkiness – a good mirror of how Puck is.**

THE GROUPS AND THEIR LANGUAGE
TEACHERS' VERSION

Solution (pages 47-48)

The character's words	What does the poetic form tell us about the character?
PUCK (talking to Oberon in Act III Scene 2) Near to her close and consecrated bower, While she was in her dull and sleeping hour, A crew of patches, rude Mechanicals, That work for bread upon Athenian stalls, Were met together to rehearse a play, Intended for great Theseus' nuptial day.	**What can you say about the rhythm and rhyme?** **5 stresses per line – pure (with exception of "Theseus") iambic pentameter. Once again the lines rhyme as rhyming couplets.**
	What effect does this mode of speaking have? **Puck is more serious here; he is, after all, talking to his master. Although he cannot suppress his rhyme and the speeding of one line into the next, the five stresses give his lines a more serious tone.**
MECHANICALS	
PETER QUINCE (talking to the Mechanicals in Act I Scene 2) Here is the scroll of every man's name, which is thought fit, through all Athens, to play in our interlude before the duke and the duchess, on his wedding-day at night.	**What can you say about the rhythm and rhyme?** **There is neither rhythm nor rhyme in this – this is prose.**
	What effect does this mode of speaking have? **Prose – as a more pedestrian way of speaking – suits the Mechanicals. They are simple people, so they speak simply, in prose rather than in verse like all the other characters.**
BOTTOM (as Pyramus in the play, Act V Scene 1) But stay, O spite! But mark, poor knight, What dreadful dole is here? Eyes, do you see? How can it be? O dainty duck! O dear! Thy mantle good, What! stain'd with blood? Approach, ye Furies fell! O Fates, come, come; Cut thread and thrum; Quail, crush, conclude, and quell!	**What can you say about the rhythm and rhyme?** **Lines with 2 stresses alternate with lines of 3 stresses, all iambs. The lines rhyme (rhyming couplets).**
	What effect does this mode of speaking have? **The lines are so short, they cannot build meaning well and therefore sound more like bursts than real speech. In addition the rhymes are quite simple, which – together with the rhythm and line length – makes this sound quite ridiculous. This suits the Mechanicals' play, which is meant to sound ridiculous.**
LOVERS	
HERMIA (talking to Lysander in Act I Scene 1) I swear to thee, by Cupid's strongest bow, By his best arrow with the golden head, By the simplicity of Venus' doves, By that which knitteth souls and prospers loves, And by that fire which burn'd the Carthage queen, When the false Trojan under sail was seen, By all the vows that ever men have broke, In number more than ever women spoke: In that same place thou hast appointed me, To-morrow truly will I meet with thee.	**What can you say about the rhythm and rhyme?** **5 stresses per line: iambic pentameter (pure). Although her initial speech does not rhyme, as she professes her love for Lysander, Hermia starts to rhyme.**
	What effect does this mode of speaking have? **Depending on the subject matter, the lovers sometimes rhyme, sometimes don't. Here, the rhyme softens the gravity of the pentameter and makes the lines softer, and they cling together more. The pentameter shows she is careful in what she says and talks in a considered manner. She is therefore a lover who is intellectually in control of the situation.**

ANTITHESIS
TEACHERS' VERSION

Solution (page 49)

LYSANDER

The course of true love never did run smooth;

But, either it was different in blood,--

HERMIA

O cross! too **high** to be enthrall'd to <u>low</u>!

LYSANDER

Or else misgraffed in respect of years,--

HERMIA

O spite! too **old** to be engag'd to <u>young</u>!

HELENA

O, that your **frowns** would teach my <u>smiles</u> such skill!

HERMIA

I give him <u>curses</u>, yet he gives me **love**.

HELENA

O, that my prayers could such affection move!

HERMIA

The more I **hate**, the more he <u>follows</u> me.

HELENA

The more I **love**, the more he <u>hateth</u> me.

BOTTOM'S "BOTTOMISMS"
TEACHERS' VERSION

Solution (page 50)

	What word should he have used?	What does the word he has used mean?
You were best to call them generally, man by man (I.2)	individually or severally	as a whole group, involving all
but I will aggravate my voice so, that I will roar you as gently as any sucking dove (I.2)	moderate	make worse / make more harsh
and there we may rehearse, most obscenely and courageously (I.2)	seemingly (may be inspired by them acting scenes)	in an indecent or disgusting way
he himself must speak through, saying thus, or to the same defect, (III.1)	effect	shortcoming or imperfection
or else one must [...] and say, he comes to disfigure, or to present, the person of Moonshine (III.1 – Quince)	figure	spoil the appearance of
I have an exposition of sleep come upon me (IV.1)	disposition to	a full description and explanation of something; a large public showing of art
Since lion vile hath here deflower'd my dear (V.1)	devoured	to deflower is to take away the virginity of a woman, often against her will

THE LOVERS' (AND OTHERS') INSULTS
TEACHERS' VERSION

Solution (page 53)

Hermia vs. Demetrius
Out, dog! Out, cur! (III.2, 66)

Hermia vs. Helena
You juggler! You canker-blossom! You thief of love! (III.2, 284-5) thou painted maypole (III.2, 298)

Demetrius vs. Lysander
Thou runaway, thou coward (III.2, 407)

Lysander vs. Hermia

Away, you Ethiope! (III.2, 259)

Hang off, thou cat, thou burr! Vile thing, let loose (III.2, 262)

Out, tawny Tartar, out! Out loathed medicine! O hated potion, hence! (III.2, 265-6)

Get you gone, you dwarf; you minimus, of hindering knot-grass made; you bead, you acorn. (III.2,330-3)

Helena vs. Hermia

Injurious Hermia! Most ungrateful maid! (III.2, 196)

You counterfeit, you puppet, you! (III.2, 290)

She was a vixen, when she went to school (III.2, 326)

Who is insulting whom?	The insult
Egeus vs. Lysander	Scornful Lysander! (I.1, 91)
Titania vs. Oberon	What, jealous Oberon! (II.1, 61)
Oberon vs. Titania	Ill met by moonlight, proud Titania. (II.1, 60) Tarry, rash wanton. (II.1, 63)

EXPLORING ACT 1 SCENE 1
TEACHERS' VERSION

Solution (page 55)

Themes	Evidence from the text	Explain relevance of evidence
Love & Marriage	Theseus announces he will marry Hippolyta in four days; he won her in war and intends to make her love him through pomp.	The nuptials of Theseus are the backdrop for the whole play. It provides the reason for the Mechanicals' play. His marriage is one aspect of marriage – the state wedding, which has little to do with love.
	Egeus wants Hermia to marry his choice of husband although she is in love with someone else.	Marriage here seems to run counter to love, and we have here the makings of a tragedy (cf. *Romeo & Juliet* and *Pyramus & Thisbe*) if not for the events in the wood.
Obedience	Theseus, as ruler of Athens, expects obedience from his subjects, and Egeus reinforces this: "with duty and desire we follow you".	Theseus eventually overrules Egeus – but is also prepared to do what he must. Obedience goes both ways. Without strict obedience the world would end in chaos, as shown by the quarrel of Titania and Oberon.
	Hermia is not prepared to submit to her father and actually wishes him to obey her: "I would my father looked but with my eyes"	Love is stronger than any other bonds. That she is willing to risk everything for love leads to the lovers being in the woods. She is obedient to love (once again this could lead to tragedy as in *Pyramus & Thisbe*).
	Lysander and Hermia plan to escape the laws of Athens and thus the need to obey Theseus's injunction.	Obedience cannot be given when it goes against fundamental personal feeling. The only solution seems to be to flee.
Dreams	Hippolyta says about the wait till they are married, "Four nights will quickly dream away the time".	Dreams are entertaining and while away the time – the whole play can be seen as a dream (cf. the epilogue).
	Dreams belong to love, as do thoughts and sighs.	Suggests that lovers and dreamers are connected – as we shall see: the antics of the lovers seem to be dreams to them.
Imagination (the mind's eye)	Hermia wants her father to see Lysander with her eyes (and Theseus tells her she must see Demetrius with her father's eyes).	That beauty is in the eye of the beholder is a cliché that is particularly relevant to the play. The flower's juice has to be smeared into the eye, underlining how eyesight is altered by love.
	Helen wishes she were "Hermia's fair" rather than her own fair, as Demetrius is attracted to the former.	Once again shows there is no impartiality in love and that beauty is subjective. This will be played out in detail in the woods as both men's perceptions are altered by the flower.
	Helena muses on love and the fact that Cupid is blind.	This is true not only of the lovers, but in particular of Titania, who does not truly see whom she has fallen in love with.

HAPPY EVER AFTER?
TEACHERS' VERSION

Solution (page 57)

Couple	Will they live on happily?	Evidence from the text
Theseus & Hippolyta	They will stay married, but whether happily or not is less easy to predict. She loves her freedom, so will not enjoy the confines of marriage. Theseus seems intent on pleasing her, so the beginning should be happy. However, Theseus is a philanderer, and therefore it seems likely that in time he will wander and she will grow frustrated and go hunting on her own; maybe she will have affairs, too.	Hippolyta does not have a large role but seems to accept her situation (I.1), suggesting the marriage – as a state affair – will stay. Speech about hounds suggests she misses hunting and the freedom of it (IV.1). Theseus refers to her frequently (I.1, IV.1). Oberon lists Theseus's lovers in Act II Scene 1.
Lysander & Hermia	They will be happy as they seem devoted to each other and genuinely love one another. The episode in the woods may linger on and lead to awkward questions later, but both seem happy to accept that as a dream.	Both were prepared to run away together and build a new life away from Athens (I.1). Lysander immediately returns to Hermia and does not seem to miss Helena on waking (IV.1). Hermia never believed Lysander would forsake her of his own will (III.1 and 2), so she trusts him.
Demetrius & Helena	Possibly, but not as assured as Lysander and Hermia: Demetrius, thanks to the potion, cannot do anything but dote on her. Although Helena reciprocates this feeling, it is not clear how she will deal with a clinging Demetrius later in life. She will fall out of love and maybe learn to love Demetrius, but will she be able to put up with a continually doting Demetrius?	Demetrius can but dote (III.2 and II.1); Helena also dotes on him (I.1 and II.1). Doting (the feeling of being in love) usually gives way to more mature love; with Demetrius it can't. This could be a source of later problems, as Helena, when she dotes, is barely tolerable to ordinary humans (II.1).
Oberon & Titania	The two seem reconciled. Their love and passion for one another was never in doubt, so as king and queen they will be happy. However, it is to be expected that they will continue to have spats and disagree quite forcefully, making up again soon afterward.	Reconciliation in Act IV Scene 1. Oberon's continued passion is evident in Act IV Scene 1, too. Oberon is "jealous," and he is intent on having Titania obey him (II.1). She is independent of him and a power in her own right (II.1 and III.1). Further conflicts therefore seem inevitable.

LYSANDER LOVES AND DOTES
TEACHERS' VERSION

Solution (page 58)

Lysander loves Hermia	Lysander dotes on Helena
Act I Scene 1: Lysander plans to escape from Athens: 　　　therefore, hear me, Hermia. I have a widow aunt, a dowager Of great revenue, and she hath no child: From Athens is her house remote seven leagues; And she respects me as her only son. There, gentle Hermia, may I marry thee, And to that place the sharp Athenian law Cannot pursue us. If thou lov'st me then, Steal forth thy father's house to-morrow night, And in the wood, a league without the town (Where I did meet thee once with Helena, To do observance to a morn of May), There will I stay for thee.	Act II Scene 2: Lysander wakes to fall in love with Helena and then explains why he loves her now: And run through fire I will for thy sweet sake. Transparent Helena! Nature here shows art, That through thy bosom makes me see thy heart. [...] Content with Hermia! No; I do repent The tedious minutes I with her have spent. Not Hermia, but Helena I love. Who will not change a raven for a dove? The will of man is by his reason sway'd; And reason says you are the worthier maid. [...] Reason becomes the marshal to my will, And leads me to your eyes; where I o'erlook Love's stories, written in love's richest book.
Act II Scene 2: Lysander and Hermia are lost in the wood and they decide to rest. He tries to sleep next to Hermia: Fair love, you faint with wand'ring in the wood; And, to speak troth, I have forgot our way: We'll rest us, Hermia, if you think it good, And tarry for the comfort of the day. [...] O, take the sense, sweet, of my innocence! Love takes the meaning in love's conference. I mean, that my heart unto yours is knit. So that but one heart we can make of it: Two bosoms interchained with an oath; So then, two bosoms, and a single troth. Then, by your side no bed-room me deny; For, lying so, Hermia, I do not lie.	Act III Scene 2: Lysander is still trying to persuade Helena that he loves her more than Demetrius, who also dotes on Helena now: And yours of Helena to me bequeath, Whom I do love, and will do till my death. [...] Fair Helena, who more engilds the night Than all you fiery oes and eyes of light. [...] Stay, gentle Helena! hear my excuse: [...] Helen, I love thee; by my life, I do: I swear by that which I will lose for thee, To prove him false, that says I love thee not.

LYSANDER LOVES AND DOTES
TEACHERS' VERSION

Solution (page 58 cont'd)

Lysander loves Hermia	Lysander dotes on Helena
How does he address each woman?	
Hermia, gentle Hermia, fair love, sweet	transparent Helena, fair Helena, gentle Helena, Helen
Comparison: While the names appear to be very similar, what Lysander calls Hermia seems to focus more on character (sweet, gentle), and Helena's appellations focus more on her looks (transparent, fair). Both are called gentle, and this may be to calm them rather than as a marker of their character. Furthermore, the "fair" he calls both could in one case be applied to character (Hermia), in the other to looks (Helena), as the love potion bewitches his eyes.	
What imagery does he use? What for?	
When planning the escape he uses very straightforward language – this is administration rather than lovers' talk. When trying to persuade Hermia, his language becomes more metaphorical with images of true love: hearts knitted and chained together.	His language is exaggerated and full of imagery, mainly comparing Helena to other natural phenomena and finding them wanting. He uses a lot of comparatives and superlatives, too.
Comparison: When talking to Hermia, Lysander's language is mainly quite plain, although he does employ (quite clever, but commonplace) metaphors when trying to persuade her. This may have to do with the fact that the wooing is over and they are secure in each other's love, making 'flowery' language unnecessary. With Helena, Lysander has to try to convince her of his love, and he uses hyperbole for this and an excessive praise of her looks.	
Are there any differences in emotion? Explain how you can tell.	
This seems to be a more settled relationship with openness and honesty, with no need to impress or make compliments the whole time. He does not use complicated metaphors, and he talks very honestly when planning their escape. When he tries to persuade her to share a bed with him, he employs more intricate language, but this is not exaggerated.	His language is marked by frequent exclamations and "do or die" statements about his love and Helena's beauty. As such, the language does not ring as true as when Lysander is in love. One almost has the feeling he could be talking to any woman.

LOVE AND REASON
TEACHERS' VERSION

Solution (page 59)

Titania
I pray thee, gentle mortal, sing again:
Mine ear is much enamour'd of thy note;
So is mine eye enthralled to thy shape;
And thy fair virtue's force, perforce, doth move me,
On the first view to say, to swear, I love thee.

Bottom
Methinks, mistress, you should have little reason for that: and yet, to say the truth, reason and love keep little company together now-a-days; the more the pity, that some honest neighbours will not make them friends. Nay, I can gleek upon occasion.

Titania
Thou art as wise as thou art beautiful.

Bottom
Not so, neither: but if I had wit enough to get out of this wood, I have enough to serve mine own turn.

Titania
Out of this wood do not desire to go:
Thou shalt remain here, whether thou wilt or no.
I am a spirit of no common rate:
The summer still doth tend upon my state;
And I do love thee: therefore, go with me;
I'll give thee fairies to attend on thee; […]
And I will purge thy mortal grossness so,
That thou shalt like an airy spirit go.

What characteristics of Bottom does Titania say she is in love with?
His voice, his figure, and his wit / wisdom.

What tells us that she realizes he is not quite a fit companion?
She wants to make him a fairy, to "purge" his mortal roughness. This suggests that him being a mortal somehow bothers her.

How do we know Titania – though besotted – is still a powerful queen, not to be crossed?
"Thou shalt remain here" is an imperious command. She also has a fairy train which she is willing to put at his service, but which she can equally use to keep him with her.

Why is Titania's love unreasonable?
It is quite obvious that Bottom has none of the things she says she is in love with. There is therefore no sound basis for her love, making it unreasonable.

100

LOVE AND REASON
TEACHERS' VERSION

Solution (page 60)

Lysander The will of man is by his reason sway'd, And reason says you are the worthier maid. Things growing are not ripe until their season: So I, being young, till now ripe not to reason; And touching now the point of human skill, Reason becomes the marshal to my will, And leads me to your eyes; where I o'erlook Love's stories, written in love's richest book.	How does Lysander explain his change of feelings? **He has grown up. With his full faculty of reason he now knows (intellectually) that Helena is the worthier woman.**
	Why do you think he uses reason as an argument? **Reason is something very difficult to dispute. If someone argues logically, it is much harder to argue against that. Also, it sounds more serious.**
	What could you say against this argument? **Lysander won't have grown up in one night. Maturing is a process that takes time and therefore cannot account for a sudden shift in affection. Also, he does not explain the reasons for Helena being "worthier". Besides, falling in love has little to do with reason.**
Demetrius But, my good lord, I wot not by what power,– But by some power it is,– my love to Hermia, Melted as the snow, seems to me now As the remembrance of an idle gaud, Which in my childhood I did dote upon; And all the faith, the virtue of my heart, The object and the pleasure of mine eye, Is only Helena. To her, my lord, Was I betroth'd ere I saw Hermia: But, like a sickness, did I loathe this food; But, as in health, come to my natural taste, Now I do wish it, love it, long for it, And will for evermore be true to it.	How does Demetrius explain that he loves Helena once again? **On the one hand he seems to suggest, like Lysander, that he has grown up and discarded his childhood folly of Hermia. On the other, he likens his loving of Hermia to a sickness that intervened in his healthy state of loving Helena (before he became "sick with Hermia" and afterwards, having been cured by the love potion)**
	Why is the image of "sickness" particularly apt? **When doting on someone, it is often said one is lovesick. As his love for Hermia was not returned, he was, in fact, lovesick (though not in the way he now maintains).**
	What could you say against his argument? **The argument brought against Lysander about growing up can be used here as well. Furthermore, loving someone cannot be described as a sickness – it is not a bodily disposition that can easily be altered. In the end, the most one can do is say – like Demetrius – that "by some power" that must remain unknown, his love has changed. It has nothing to do with reason, growing up, or convalescing, though.**

STAR-CROSSED LOVERS
TEACHERS' VERSION

Solution (page 61)

Question:	Hermia & Lysander	Pyramus & Thisbe	Romeo & Juliet
Who is against their marriage and why?	Hermia's father, Egeus, and – because Egeus evokes the law of Athens – Theseus, Duke of Athens, their ruler, too. We don't know why Egeus is against Lysander marrying Hermia, except that he wants her to marry Demetrius.	We only know of the wall, but this suggests that both their parents are against the relationship.	Both families are against them even associating with one another, as the Montagues and Capulets are sworn enemies
How do they attempt to overcome the opposition to their love?	They agree to meet in the woods at night and then flee from Athens to a rich aunt of Lysander. They will live there, as the law of Athens does not apply in that region.	They agree to meet outside the town, at Ninus' (Ninny's!) tomb. We do not know whether this was merely to be able to meet one another or whether they planned to elope.	They marry in secret and plan on leaving Verona with the help of Friar Laurence. He puts Juliet into a death-like sleep and plans on getting her to Romeo that way.
Does the plan work?	Because of Helena, they are followed into the woods by Lysander's rival in love, Demetrius. They also lose their way and are discovered the next morning by Theseus and Egeus – so superficially, the plan does not work.	Thisbe is first at the tomb and runs away as a lion is there. It mauls her mantle. Pyramus finds it and, believing Thisbe has been killed by a lion, kills himself. Thisbe finds his body and kills herself too.	Romeo is not told of the plan, and on seeing Juliet he believes her truly dead, so he kills himself. Juliet wakes up to find Romeo dead and kills herself as well.
What is the outcome?	Hermia and Lysander marry, as Demetrius gives up his claim to Hermia, and Theseus then overrules Egeus.	The lovers are both dead (both having committed suicide).	The lovers are both dead (both having committed suicide).
What is the main reason for this outcome?	Demetrius gives up his claim to Hermia as he magically falls in love with Helena, due to the magic flower juice.	The lion, forcing Pyramus to jump to the wrong conclusion.	The letter of Friar Laurence to tell Romeo of the plan did not reach him (so Friar John, the messenger, is at fault).

WHO MUST OBEY WHOM?
TEACHERS' VERSION

Solution (page 63)

Fill in the names of the following characters in the chart below and show how obedience and dominance are displayed in the play.

Hermia, Puck, Lysander, Demetrius, Titania, Hippolyta, Theseus, Oberon, Egeus

The Athenians

Theseus
Marries Hippolyta to subjugate her; orders Hermia to obey her father and ordains that all lovers will be wedded with him.

Hippolyta
Does not complain of her role and seems to accept Theseus's dominance.

Egeus
Seeks Theseus's protection, carries out his orders and lets himself be overruled.

Lysander
Accepts the common nuptials but is not prepared to accept his ruling concerning Hermia.

Demetrius
Accepts all of Theseus's rulings and is prepared to carry out his work.

Hermia
At beginning owes obedience to father, which she refuses, as it goes against her feelings. After marriage, owes obedience to Lysander.

The Fairies

Oberon
Orders Puck around and makes Titania pay for disobeying him.

Puck
Jests for Oberon and also carries out his will concerning the lovers.

Titania
Refuses to obey Oberon to give him the changeling; when punished, accepts her role as his queen.

103

I SPY WITH MY LITTLE EYE
TEACHERS' VERSION

Solution (page 65)

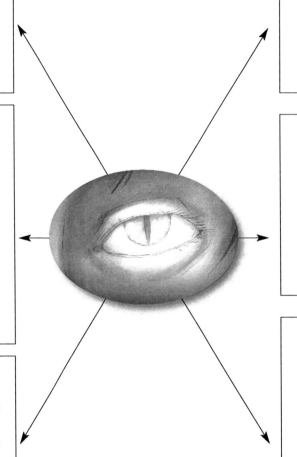

Hermia
Theseus asks her to look with her father's eyes and see Demetrius as a worthy husband. The fact that she refuses leads all the lovers into the woods.

Demetrius
a) Helena wishes he could see her with the eyes of all of Athens, who deem her fair (l.1).
b) Due to the love potion, he sees Helena with the eyes of doting, which leads to the two marrying. This paves the way for Hermia and Lysander to marry.

The Athenian Court
The Mechanicals ask them to believe the wall is a real wall, the lion not a lion, and that a man is the man in the moon. The irony is that they do not trust the audience's imagination.

Lysander
Due to the love potion, he looks with the eyes of doting on Helena. This leads to chaos and confusion (and comedy) in the woods. This change is reversed.

Titania
Due to the love potion, she looks with the eyes of doting on the ass-headed Bottom. This makes her give up the changeling boy and reconciles Oberon to her.

Egeus
Hermia asks him to look with her eyes to see that Lysander is as worthy a husband as Demetrius. His refusal leads to Hermia's flight and to Theseus overruling him at the end, ultimately allowing Hermia to marry Lysander.

WHO IS DREAMING WHAT?
TEACHERS' VERSION

Solution (page 66)

Who does the dream apply to?	Evidence from the text & content of the dream	Relevance of the dream
Theseus (I.1)	"Four nights will quickly dream away the time" The content of the dream is unknown – the purpose is that the four long nights that Theseus is bemoaning until his wedding will pass quickly, as he will dream – shortening the time.	As the play covers the time until the wedding and is titled "Dream," it seems that in a certain way a dream does shorten the time until the wedding. Also, to shorten the time until the wedding night, Theseus watches a play – "shadows" – which is reminiscent of a dream.
Hermia (II.2)	"What a dream was here! ... Methought a serpent ate my heart away, / And you sat smiling at his cruel prey" Hermia, left alone by Lysander, dreams a snake slithered onto her breast to eat her heart, and Lysander, her love, did nothing to stop it.	This is the only real dream in the play. The dream seems to warn Hermia that Lysander has gone. The snake is an image of cunning that hurts her heart; it is cunning (Helena's art – so she believes) that lures Lysander away from her, leaving her heart wounded. As such the dream is not accurate, but possibly it is due to this dream that Hermia later blames Helena for having stolen Lysander from her.
Lovers (IV.1)	"May all to Athens back again repair, / And think no more of this night's accidents / But as the fierce vexation of a dream" (Oberon) "and by the way let us recount our dreams" (Demetrius) On waking the morning after the goings-on in the woods, the lovers all have the feeling they have been dreaming.	Oberon foretells that the lovers will believe all that happened to them was a dream (does he enchant them?). Indeed, this is what happens, probably because seeing it all as a dream is the easiest way to deal with it. If it was all a dream, Lysander can avoid searching questions from Hermia about his crush on Helena, and Helena and Hermia's friendship can remain intact. In this sense it is a *deus ex machina* solution (like at the end of a lot of pupils' stories: "Then I woke up: it was all a dream").

WHO IS DREAMING WHAT?
TEACHERS' VERSION

Solution (page 67)

Who does the dream apply to?	Evidence from the text & content of the dream	Relevance of the dream
Bottom (IV.1)	"I have had a most rare vision" Bottom thinks his experience with Titania has all been a dream. To what extent he ever realized he had an ass's head on is open to debate.	The dream quality here has more to do with the absolute unreality of what he has been through: being transformed and also the lover of the fairy queen. This puts encounters with fairies safely in the realm of dreams – meaning one doesn't have to deal with them. The experience does not seem to have changed him.
Titania (IV.1)	"My Oberon! what visions have I seen!" When woken from her trance induced by the love potion, she thinks that her loving a donkey was nothing but a dream.	Oberon shows Titania Bottom with the donkey's head, and she realizes she has not been dreaming (she is the only affected character to realize that the happenings have not been a dream). This probably shocks her as it means there is no easy way to deal with what has happened. Titania realizes how far Oberon is prepared to go to get his own way and is reconciled to him.
Audience (epilogue)	"And this weak and idle theme, / No more yielding but a dream" The whole play should be seen as having no more importance than a dream, if the audience is not pleased with it.	This is a somewhat puzzling request, as it calls into question the whole play and what Shakespeare is trying to tell us. On the other hand, the play is called "A Dream". Saying it should be seen as no more important than a dream makes us wonder what kind of dream – dreams can be taken very seriously as a reflection of the dreamer's psyche (or, in a more Elizabethan vein, as a prophetic vision). Also, if the play was all a dream, perhaps Shakespeare is suggesting our whole lives are but dreams – a thought elaborated in the film *The Matrix.*

CHASTE DIANA
TEACHERS' VERSION

Solution (page 69)

Extract	What does the extract mean?
Theseus, bewailing the fact that time passes too slowly until his wedding day (I.1) but, O, methinks, how slow This old moon wanes! She lingers my desires, Like to a step-dame, or a dowager, Long withering out a young man's revenue.	He suggests the moon (representing chastity, possibly) does not want him to marry quickly. The moon is like an old woman preventing a young man achieving his desire (i.e. marrying) by drawing out the moment he will receive his inheritance (enabling him to marry).
Theseus, describing to Hermia what fate awaits her, should she disobey her father (I.1) For aye to be in shady cloister mew'd, To live a barren sister all your life, Chanting faint hymns to the cold fruitless moon.	The adjectives used here have a strong negative connotation: it is obvious that for Theseus, living life as a nun is but a pale reflection of what a woman should do in life – marry. "Faint hymns" suggest that the songs are ineffective; a sentiment repeated by the "fruitless moon". Basically, Theseus is saying that as a nun, Hermia would fulfill no purpose and be wasted.
Oberon, describing how the flower "love-in-idleness" gained its power from Cupid's arrow (II.1) And loos'd his love-shaft smartly from his bow, As it should pierce a hundred thousand hearts. But I might see young Cupid's fiery shaft Quench'd in the chaste beams of the wat'ry moon	Oberon is describing how the flower received its power: Cupid was aiming at a fair virgin (often thought to be a reference to Elizabeth I), but the arrow was ineffectual, the chaste moon having put out its fire and thus its power to make the virgin fall in love. Here the moon is being called chaste, reinforcing the imagery of chastity. The fiery shaft quenched is like the dousing of ardent love in cold indifference, the quenching being reinforced by the "watery" moon – the cold shower that extinguishes strong desire.
Titania, enamored, before she retires with Bottom (III.1) The moon, methinks, looks with a watery eye; And when she weeps, weeps every little flower, Lamenting some enforced chastity.	Here the chaste moon spreads dew on the land, which is seen as it crying. Titania, her lover in her arm, says the moon is crying because it is forced to remain chaste, when obviously all else is attuned to love. The phrase is ambiguous, though, and could also mean that the moon is weeping because its chastity has been violated. This double-meaning would fit in the sense that Titania's loyal love to Oberon (marital chastity) has been violated by her being forced to fall in love with Bottom.
Oberon, applying the cure for the love potion into Titania's eyes (IV.1) Be, as thou wast wont to be; See, as thou wast wont to see: Dian's bud o'er Cupid's flower Hath such force and blessed power.	Oberon seems to pronounce that chastity (Dian's bud) is stronger than the folly of love (Cupid's flower). Chastity is here seen as a positive trait that carries with it the power to resist love (as in II.1, above). For Titania it suggests a return to "chastity" (marital fidelity) from her night of mad doting on a monster, suggesting a connection to the moon goddess.

THESEUS'S SPEECH ON LOVERS, POETS AND MADMEN
TEACHERS' VERSION

Solution (page 70)

Why would a madman see devils? What connotation does this give to the madman?
This makes madmen seem more evil and apart from God – it makes them outcasts of society (which may reflect on lovers and poets, too).

Note the many references to eyes and seeing – how does this relate to the rest of the play?
Theseus suggests that the three groups see with their own eyes and do not see what "normal" people see, but only what they imagine.

Does "cool reason" sound positive or negative? Explain.
Cool reason is devoid of emotion, but it sounds quite detached and not desirable. We prefer warmth to cold or cool. So, in a way, Theseus is possibly not entirely convinced of his argument.

Who is the Helen being referred to here? The one from the play, or another? Why Egypt?
Although Helena is called Helen by both Lysander and Demetrius, Theseus is referring to Helen of Troy, renowned for her beauty. Here, he is comparing her against one of dark-skinned complexion, thought in Shakespeare's day to be unattractive.

What does the poet do with his pen?
He makes up imaginary places, people and creatures, and makes them seem like they really exist.

Is the poet more like the lover or the madman?
As the poet creates and sees things others don't, whereas the lover only changes how they see others, it seems the poet is more like a madman – seeing things that aren't there.

Do these last lines refer to poets only or to all three? Explain.
This is unclear. Could refer only to the poet, but could also refer to all three, making the bond between them closer. The two lines ending in "joy" could easily apply to lovers, too. The last two lines could be a reference to the *Pyramus and Thisbe* story, where the lovers are interrupted by a wild beast.

What do the words "frantic" and "fine frenzy" suggest?
That the three are almost in a fever, in a heightened state of emotions and thought, that possibly produces the visions.

CHARACTERISTIC ONE-LINERS
TEACHERS' VERSION

Solution (page 77)

Theseus	But, O, methinks, how slow this old moon wanes
Hippolyta	I never heard so musical a discord, such sweet thunder
Egeus	I beg the ancient privilege of Athens
Oberon	Thou shalt not from this grove, till I torment thee for this injury
Titania	The fairyland buys not the child of me
Robin Goodfellow	I am that merry wanderer of the night
Bottom	If I do it, let the audience look to their eyes
Quince	But, masters, here are your parts
Flute	Nay, faith, let me not play a woman; I have a beard coming
Starveling	All that I have to say, is, to tell you that the lantern is the moon; I, the man i' the moon
Snout	You can never bring in a wall
Snug	Have you the lion's part written? pray you, if it be, give it me, for I am slow of study
Helena	I will fawn on you: use me but as your spaniel
Hermia	I know not by what power I am made bold
Lysander	I am, my lord, as well deriv'd as he
Demetrius	I love thee not, therefore pursue me not

WORD JUMBLE
TEACHERS' VERSION

Solution (page 81)

Slay nerd	Lysander
Tiered Sum	Demetrius
She Suet	Theseus
Happy Toil	Hippolyta
He I Mar	Hermia
An Heel	Helena
She Tan	Athens
Hotplate Sir	Philostrate
Ron Beo	Oberon
I At A Nit	Titania
Wool Go Fled	Goodfellow
To Tomb	Bottom
Nic Que	Quince
Grist V Lane	Starveling
Guns	Snug
Not Us	Snout
Clang Hinge	Changeling
Seated Drums	Mustardseed
Lame Boss Pose	Peaseblossom
Ebb Cow	Cobweb
DI Puc	Cupid
Ms Mire Mud	Midsummer
Things	Nights
Armed	Dream
She Peaks Ear	Shakespeare

CROSSWORD
TEACHERS' VERSION

Solution (page 82)

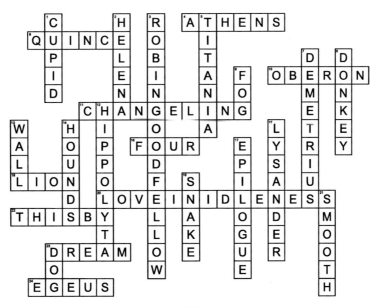

109

WORD SEARCH
TEACHERS' VERSION

Solution (page 83)

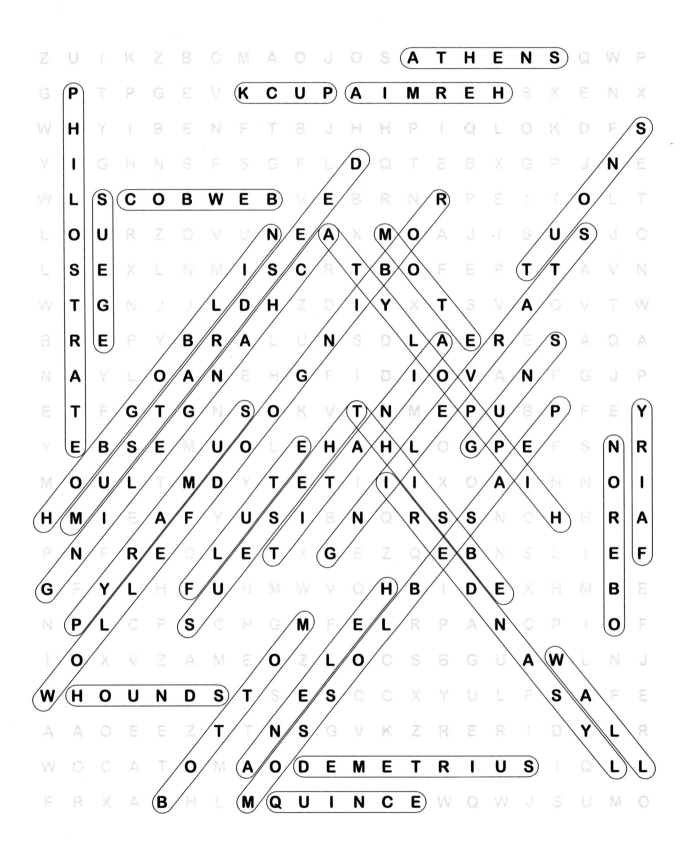